Afterbirth

Afterbirth

Stories You Won't Read in a Parenting Magazine

EDITED BY

Dani Klein Modisett

ST. MARTIN'S PRESS

New York

www.stmartins.com

ISBN-13: 978-0-312-56714-9
ISBN-10: 0-312-56714-6

First Edition: May 2009

10 9 8 7 6 5 4 3 2 1

COPYRIGHT ACKNOWLEDGMENTS

For my parents, Muriel and Victor,
who gave me the freedom to make mistakes
and the courage to laugh about them

CONTENTS

Contents

Contents

ACKNOWLEDGMENTS

THERE WOULD BE NO BOOK without my husband, Tod Modisett. Tod does not believe in quitting. So I didn't.

There would also be no book without the impressive courage and excessive talent of each of the contributors to all of the *Afterbirth* shows over the last five years. The writers, actors, comics, and musicians who have performed on *Afterbirth* always surprise me and make me want to be a better writer. And a better mother.

There are several other people to whom I am indebted for their guidance and support. These include, but are not limited to, Elizabeth Beier, my champion and editor, in that order; Elisabeth Weed, the classiest agent I've ever met; Claudette Sutherland, my teacher; Adam Peck, my partner in crime on all things literary and theatrical; Rachel Ekstrom, my publicist at St. Martin's; Linda Benjamin, Caroline Aaron, Dan Bucatinsky, Cindy Chupack, and Barbara Hoffman; my aunt Thelma, for always telling me that what I really am is a writer;

Acknowledgments

most of the parents at Temple Israel of Hollywood Nursery School and Day School; Theresa Maganna; Deborah Townsend; Cedering Fox; and, I really can't stress this enough, my mother, Muriel Klein.

I would also like to thank Joe Reynolds at M Bar in Hollywood and John and all the waiters and bartenders there and at the Triad Theater in New York City, for being gracious, efficient, and quiet.

Afterbirth

PROLOGUE

I NEVER PLANNED ON HAVING children. It's not like I planned on *not* having children, I just never gave it much thought at all. I'd heard of other girls who dreamed about their weddings and having babies, but not me. No surprise. Once, when I was a little girl, I asked my father if he was happy having just my sister and me, or if he was disappointed that he never had a son, to which he promptly responded, "What do I need a son for? I have you."

Then I went to a predominantly male college and became a stand-up comic, a field where men still outnumber women 100 to 1, or so it feels. Consequently, being a mother was not something I thought about. Until my father was diagnosed with terminal cancer and my sister got pregnant with her first child. I was touring then, and I remember doing jokes about how I was raised by my parents to be a career woman but since my sister had gotten pregnant the game in my family had suddenly changed from Monopoly to Mr. Potato Head. Now instead of amassing power and money, I was supposed to find a man and have a baby. It wasn't a great joke because it always required an explanation. My point was that despite how much my father had pushed me to succeed in my work, on his deathbed what really mattered to him was having children and being near them. The most sustaining aspect of my father's life at that time, keeping him alive longer than predicted, was being able to hold his tiny granddaughter. After he passed away, not only did I grieve his death, but I was also completely unnerved having seen that in the end, it is family that matters most.

I immediately packed up and moved three thousand miles away from anyone who was related to me and still breathing.

I MET MY HUSBAND AT a party a year later. He was nine years younger than me, shaved his head, and drank heavily. He didn't exactly scream "mate." Nevertheless, through a few ups and downs he turned out to be exactly the right man for me. We married in October 2001. Four months later Oprah, *Time* magazine, and *Newsweek* (in response to Sylvia Ann Hewlett's book *Creating a Life: Professional Women and the Quest for Children*) threw a massive floodlight on how devastatingly unlikely it is for women over thirty-five to get pregnant with ease. I remember sitting with my mother in one of those cramped Upper East Side restaurants during this fertility frenzy. We were sandwiched in between two tables of single women going on and on about their predicaments.

"I'm not even dating anyone," I heard to my left.

"My boyfriend's a musician! He can't even take care of a plant!" came at me from the right, followed by, "I'm thirty-five right now, that is so old, what am I going to do?"

I pushed my plate away. I was thirty-seven, what was *I* going to do? I flew home the next day, and assaulted my husband at the airport.

"We have to get pregnant now! *Tonight.*"

"Honey, calm down."

"No! We have to, it could take years, we have to at least try. Haven't you been watching *Oprah?*" (A dumb question.) "Okay, well, what about *Time* or *Newsweek?* Everyone is talking about this!"

We had sex au naturel that night, not to make a baby per se, because Tod was still convinced we should see a financial planner first, but really just to blow off steam. The following is what happened as a result of my hysteria. It is also the very first story written for what would become my show, *Afterbirth ... Stories You Won't Read in* Parents *Magazine.*

Dear Fetus,

When I got into the car that Sunday morning last July, I had this momentary lapse of control. I couldn't remember names or attach words to images. I drove home cautiously. The light was really bright. I felt like I was inside a video game. When I opened the door, I scared your father 'cause I couldn't remember his name. Tom? Ted? Tod. He took me to the ER and they wanted to take pictures of my brain but I said no, because we were invited to a fancy wedding in Bel Air that night, and I refused to be a no-show. Plus there would definitely be delicious cake. There'll always be another CAT scan, I told myself. I went home and threw on something black, and by 6:30 we were sitting in wedding-white outdoor chairs. By 10:00 P.M. my headache was so bad I told your father we had to leave. They hadn't even wheeled the cake out yet, so he knew I was serious.

It was another thirty-six hours before my head actually went numb. The next morning I went to see my doctor at the Bob Hope Health Center, a name that just screams medical integrity. Dr. Waxler then sent me for that previously intrusive CAT scan. I drove to a lab in Beverly Hills where they laid me on a metal table and pricked me with a needle of iodine.

In a few seconds it felt as if my body had been shot full of hot whiskey. It seemed to rush between my legs first, which was, surprisingly, not entirely unpleasant.

The next morning at nine my doctor from the clinic called to tell me there was an abnormality on the negative from the CAT scan and I had to have another test. The aberration was on the right side of my head. Maybe it was nothing, but maybe it was an aneurysm and maybe there was blood leaking into my brain. I hung up the phone and made an appointment to have an MRI that afternoon at five.

I decided to soldier on with my day and continued my morning ritual of staring at the computer trying to write jokes. Nothing. Not unusual. What *was* unusual was the tingling sensation creeping up the right side of my head. Like when your foot starts to come back after falling asleep. I quickly deduced that this was from the blood leaking into my brain. I didn't watch medical shows, but I knew an internal hemorrhage when I felt one.

Your father was out for a jog to try to deal with his new wife's possible impending death, so I was home alone. Suddenly, I didn't want to die that way, brain first. In retrospect I don't know why. Is there a better way to die? I called my doctor and he told me I was panicking. So I hung up on him. Fuck him, my head was tingling. (Even in trauma I have very good access to my rage.) Then I called 911. It really works! A few seconds later

I started to hear a siren in my head. I located the source. On the street. Outside my apartment. At this point, because I could still see, hear, and breathe, I started to feel really guilty. This was Los Angeles, after all, there were probably Bloods bleeding somewhere who needed attention. No time for second-guessing—the paramedics jumped out of the ambulance: a muscled black man, a reed-thin white guy with a goatee and a clipboard, and another white guy with a buzz cut holding a flaccid rubber tube ready to take my blood pressure. They started to pull the stretcher out. "I don't think you need that," I said at the threshold, still trying to figure out how numb my head was.

"Okay, Miss, go inside." Standing on the sidewalk in a nightgown being told to get back in the apartment by a man in uniform, for a minute I felt like Zelda Fitzgerald (my favorite "crazy lady" reference). Inside, they checked my vitals, which were embarrassingly vital. All I had was a numb head and an abnormal CAT scan. Lame.

They wouldn't leave. I showed them I could walk. I made coherent sentences.

I tried to make them laugh (something I would continue to attempt to do through four neurosurgeons, an EEG technician, a radiologist, and an internist over the next forty-eight hours, with little success), but still they refused to leave until my husband came home.

I finally reached Tod on his cell phone; his name came to me immediately, yet another indication that I was wasting everyone's time. He talked to the skinny guy. Then your father told me to go with the men in the red and white truck, so I did. As you may have figured out, he's almost ten years younger, and yet I often find myself deferring to his sound logic. Don't tell him that.

We finally got to the emergency room, although I don't remember those images well because I was lying on a gurney and high on clean mountain air. There is something magical about being prone and moving along without any effort of your own. Not worth getting an aneurysm over, but pretty cool. They delivered me to a back corner of the ER. If it were a restaurant, this would have been the bad table. My mother definitely would have had us moved. I was very cold and the arm with the needle shunt was stinging and I couldn't even tell anymore if my head was numb. Your father came soon, still in his running clothes, some mighty ugly green knee-length nylon shorts. I've never been so happy to see someone wearing tube socks.

Next I went for some picture taking of my brain. No iodine this time. It was like being trapped in a metal tube with one of those street drills that sounds like a machine gun firing in my ear. I wasn't allowed to move a muscle. When that was done, there wasn't any room for me in the ER so they parked me in the hallway. I wanted your father to go home and shower and, you know, change. He refused. He was afraid someone would accidentally whisk me away and amputate a leg. He'd read about things like that happening. . . .

That's when our lives changed forever.

"Well, we do have some new information," said Dr. Fishkin, the Jewish Paul Bunyan who runs the ER, loping toward us with a clipboard.

"Really? Okay," I said, bracing myself for the worst.

"You're pregnant," he said, pointing to a POS on a pink sheet of paper.

Pregnant? What? New life? I was just gearing up for this one to be taken. Your father and I looked at each other. Shocked. Yesterday I had taken a pregnancy test at the Bob Hope Clinic and it was negative. Apparently they gave the results to Mr. Hope himself to interpret. I mean, okay, we'd pulled the goalie (your father's expression, honey, not mine), but only for a week . . . and, and . . .

"Wow" fell out of my mouth quietly. Where was the pink stick? The swelling sound track as I tell your father the wondrous news? A bag of blood whizzed past my head on a metal pole.

"So what do we do now? With my brain?"

"We have a number of options," the specialist with Fishkin replied. "We think there's a twisted blood vessel. It's most likely harmless, but we certainly have the technology to pursue it further. With angioplasty or a spinal tap."

"Spinal tap? No way!" I blurted. They use a very big needle for that. I hate needles. *And I'm pregnant now*, I thought, *I have to think about what's good for the baby.*

Then I remembered. I had no idea what that was.

Fishkin cut into my thoughts. "Sometimes pregnancy can create a hormonal shift, which can cause a severe migraine headache creating the kind of symptoms you experienced."

Apparently becoming pregnant was such a shock to my system, it almost blew my head off.

A nurse came and wheeled me into the hallway, and I lay there in my paper dress with my legs spread waiting for someone to take me back downstairs. I just wanted to go home. If I'd lived this long with my twisted blood vessel I was willing to risk another thirty-seven years. I agreed with Fishkin that the whole numb head thing was because of you.

We are frighteningly close to meeting you now. I look forward to holding your little face in my hand and squishing your cheeks, remembering all of this and saying, "If all that craziness hadn't happened, then I wouldn't have you with your cute dimples and your delicious chubby thighs."

Don't be embarrassed, dear, that's how all mothers talk.

One more thing, honey. Your father and I have already decided we are going to be honest and not go on and on about how beautiful you are if you look like a troll. Don't worry, beauty fades. Just be funny and make us laugh. At least you kick me a lot now so I know I haven't accidentally killed you. Thank you for that. It's very comforting.

Love, Mom

My son was born ten months later back at that same hospital. It was a traumatic labor ending with an emergency C-section despite my forty weeks of prenatal yoga and forty hours of birthing music.

From the minute I saw my son, I knew I needed to have another child. Within two years it became very clear that Hewlett was not a whack job alarmist. My husband and I were not quite so lucky the second time around. I spent the *next* two years trying anything and everything to have another successful pregnancy. I will spare you the painful details, but I will confess that I didn't appreciate how easily sperm travels through a vagina until I tried to drive it across Los Angeles. During rush hour. The morning of the Oscars.

Fortunately, while harvesting my eggs and setting them up

on dates with my husband's swim team, and clumsily figuring out how to raise a toddler, I was also developing my show: *Afterbirth . . . Stories You Won't Read in* Parents *Magazine*.

Sure, I needed an artistic outlet for myself, but as the years went by, I had to admit that I was using the show for personal as much as for professional reasons. The stories I read and heard performed as part of *Afterbirth* inspired me without exception. Whether they described the heartbreak of a failed adoption, the joy of finally getting a child to sleep for more than four hours straight, or the guilt of being caught mumbling obscenities when all else fails, the courage, humor, and heart of these stories kept me going in my darkest days as a new parent.

From the very first show, I asked people to write about, more or less, "the moment you knew your life changed forever, becoming a parent." I was looking for that event or series of events that made you realize there was no going back or that this particular predicament you found yourself in would never have happened if only you'd stayed in that one-room apartment ordering in Chinese takeout for the rest of your life. What follows is a book with thirty-seven surprising, articulate, and most of all heartfelt answers to this question.

Keep this book handy. If you do, I know firsthand you will never again feel isolated and alone in the specific way in which you are screwing up your children.

BABY POWDER

Marta Ravin

I'M STANDING IN MY KITCHEN at two in the morning trying to make a bottle to soothe my wailing three-month-old. In my sleep-deprived haze I spill a large cup full of formula onto the shiny granite countertop. As I begin to wipe up the mess, I am struck by the fact that the last time I was looking at a mound of white powder on a shiny surface, it was definitely cocaine.

It wasn't like I ever had a "drug problem" per se; I was pretty much just a recreational user. I enjoyed drinking and smoking pot as much as the next gal . . . only more. Cocaine was strictly for parties, to enhance my Tae Bo workout, to motivate me to clean my apartment, and occasionally to snort off a stripper's ass during a threesome—whatever, it was the '90s. Anyway, after I got married, I slowed down the drug use quite a bit except

11

for the rare bender over Yom Kippur. (How else could I be expected to not eat or drink for twenty-four hours?) But once I got pregnant, it was a no-brainer; I would be completely clean and sober for nine months.

It wasn't a physical struggle for me to give up those vices when I was pregnant, but it definitely was a mental one. There are some women who pride themselves on not changing their social lives when they are pregnant. They still go out to parties and bars, proudly balancing a glass of seltzer and lime on their big bellies. I was not one of them. By my second month I realized that without the help of alcohol or drugs I'm shy, and not really good at small talk. Who knew? But I didn't mind. Ever since I had gotten married I didn't enjoy going out that much anyway. After all, what was the point of going to a bar if you couldn't make out with strangers?

Although I didn't drink or do drugs during my pregnancy, I still felt the need to rebel in some way. Unlike some of my other pregnant friends who wouldn't put a piece of cheese in their mouth without calling Louis Pasteur to make sure it was legit, I happily indulged in many pregnancy taboos. I ate tuna fish more than two times a week. I drank coffee daily. *And* I got my hair colored—all three trimesters! I just didn't think any of these small pleasures could be such a big deal. I mean, think about all the crack moms living in gutters who give birth to perfectly healthy four-pound babies. What was a little tuna on whole wheat going to do to my kid?

But there was one thing I did (or rather, didn't do) while I was pregnant that was truly risqué: I didn't take my prenatal vitamins. At first it was because they made my already brutal morning sickness unbearable. Yes, the same woman who could down a Xanax with a shot of tequila couldn't handle those stupid little pills. Even when they stopped making me sick, I still didn't take them. In my warped head, not taking the vitamins was my way of saying "Fuck you!" to everyone who told me life as I knew it was about to change. All those books about what to expect when you're expecting. Expect this, Dr. Spock! I didn't even tell my gynecologist the truth. She'd ask if I was taking the vitamins and I'd give my usual uh-huh. It was the same uh-huh I gave her when I was single and she asked if I was practicing safe sex. Lying to this woman was a natural reflex.

Cut to my fifth month. Other pregnant friends of mine were constantly remarking how their babies were "kicking up a storm," but I wasn't feeling anything. The baby never kicked. I started to think that maybe not taking those vitamins wasn't the best idea. I went to the doctor almost every week and told her the baby wasn't kicking, and she would hook me up to a sonogram machine and say, "Oh no, he looks fine. His heartbeat's strong. Nothing to worry about." Even though I was scared, I still didn't take the vitamins. I'm an instant gratification person; when I take a pill I expect something to happen immediately. I take a Tylenol, no more headache; Motrin, no more cramps; ecstasy, and I make out with a 350-pound bald bouncer named Lenny. His head was so soft. I just really didn't believe that those pills did anything but make me sick. But as each kickless month passed, I became paralyzed by my dirty little secret.

In my last few weeks I fessed up to my mother. Usually when I talked about pregnancy with my mom she would say something like, "I drank and smoked through both pregnancies, and you and your deaf, cross-eyed brother turned out fine." So I told her about the vitamins, making a joke about how they probably didn't even *have* vitamins back in her day. She just turned to me and grimly said, "No, Marta, we had vitamins, and I took them every day." Uh-oh. I guess 1972 wasn't as backward as my parents' orange Formica kitchen would suggest.

I started having major panic attacks. There was a constant lump in my throat, my stomach was in knots, and the waistband on my Liz Lange cords was getting tighter and tighter every day. I called my best friend, knowing she would agree with my "If crack moms can have healthy babies, so can I" theory. Even though she humored me and said I would be fine, deep down I was petrified.

Cut to the delivery room. I had a relatively easy birth (drug-assisted, of course). I had been looking forward to that epidural like a cold glass of chardonnay on a summer's day. My mom arrived right before the big event assuming she would be part of the birthing process. She carefully removed her jewelry and "scrubbed in," approaching the bed with her clean hands raised as she had seen Dr. Addison Montgomery-Shepherd do so many times on *Grey's Anatomy*. She was only slightly insulted when my doctor asked her to take a seat. Of course, she stayed involved on her cell phone, giving a play-by-play to my father, who was on the way. "Marta's pushing very hard. Max's holding her legs. I can sort of see the head. How is Marta? She seems fine. Her hair looks nice, and I think she got a pedicure."

Jonah Lazer Leinwand was born at 7:33 A.M. on March 6, 2007. He was seven pounds six ounces and perfect in every way . . . except for his foot. It was bent up and backward toward his leg. The doctor and nurses assured us it was probably nothing, but to make sure they would send an orthopedist to check it out.

The next day, after a sleepless night, two orthopedic assistants showed up to look at Jonah's foot. My husband had gone home to take a quick shower, but my mom was with me in the room when they came. The assistants started whispering to each other as they examined Jonah, then turned around to speak to us with grave looks in their eyes. The bigger one, whom I called Boris even though that was not his name, said, "The foot seems to be deformed and will most likely be that way for the rest of his life, unless he has surgery." In truth, I can't remember exactly what Boris said. But what I heard was, "You didn't take your prenatal vitamins, and now Jonah will be deformed *forever!*" My wild, selfish ways had finally caught up with me. The girl who tempted fate during her single years, mixing substances and fluids with wild abandon, then laughed at the "rules" of pregnancy, had finally gotten her comeuppance. I started to cry.

"Mom, is his foot deformed because I didn't take the vitamins?"

"No, of course not," she said. But her eyes were saying, "Yes."

They took Jonah away for X-rays. By the time my husband came back, I was a complete mess. Up until that moment I had never really made the connection that this thing I had been carrying around for months, feeding it mercury-filled tuna and depriving it of nutritious vitamins, was actually going to be a person: a little, helpless person I had already failed.

We eventually saw a specialist who told us that Jonah's foot was not "deformed." It was slightly bent but would probably straighten out on its own without surgery. Jonah's foot had been trapped under his other leg in my womb, which was why I never felt any kicking. It had nothing to do with not taking the vitamins.

That was seventeen months ago. I am happy to say that Jonah's foot is almost completely healed, and he is walking like a pro. I feel very lucky that his funky foot is the only medical problem Jonah has had so far. I actually feel lucky and blessed for many reasons. I have a loving husband who pretends that I have lost all my baby weight. A mother, who although she was horrified by the thought of breast-feeding me, offered to give a crying Jonah her own nipple one night while she was babysitting. *"What? He might enjoy it!"* And a father, who, although his idea of toys for me was a yellow legal pad and some Post-its, never forgets to buy Jonah a present before he sees him. I am blessed with love and family, and my life feels more important now than it ever did when I was single. These are the best reasons I have found for making sure the only white powder you'll find on my kitchen counter will be formula . . . or maybe a little heroin—but only for playdates.

THE BEST I CAN

Dana Gould

WE HAVE TWO DAUGHTERS, THREE years old and fifteen months. They are both from China. When we first announced to our friends that we were adopting from China, one person asked, "Are you going to teach her English?"

The question hung in the air like a day-old balloon before I cleared my throat and calmly answered, "No."

I didn't mean it, obviously. But, as I've gotten older, I've picked up a neat little trick. In the old days, before I was a parent, if someone said something so obviously ill conceived, I would frown, feign ignorance, and, Matlock-style, pepper them with questions designed to force a confrontation with the folly of their verbal flatulence. Then I would smile benevolently and escort them back into the sunshine of my thinking.

But now I'm too busy. Now, when someone drops a dumb-bomb, I calculate how much time it will take to disagree and argue with that person, then agree with them and use that time later in the day to treat myself to an ice cream sandwich.

We adopted from China for several reasons. As you probably know, there exists in China the so-called One Child Policy, whereby, to stem the tide of overpopulation, all families are limited to one child. For cultural reasons, male children are favored over female children, and as a result, many, many young girls are discarded.

The One Child Policy is a great idea in the long run, if your goal is to have an entire generation of men who can't meet a girl but do have access to nuclear weapons. For this reason, I am investing all of my money in the new Las Vegas–Beijing Hooker Channel. Look for our slogan: "Sending sex workers through the Earth's core to give you one more sunrise."

(Understand the details, ramifications, and my genuine feelings about this policy have no place in a comedic essay, so let's just check our inner-NPR-ness here and continue on with that in mind.)

Here's another mind-boggling question I'm asked way too much. People walk up and ask me, point-blank, "Why did you adopt your baby?" They ask me this even if I don't know them, even if I am holding the baby in question.

It's a phenomenally personal question, but I get it all the time. I don't understand this. I don't walk up to people with biological children and ask, "So, what happened here? Did your husband come home drunk and stuff his junk in your business? Did he have a couple too many and dump a load of tot nog in the baby bunker? Did you make that small human in your guts?"

That said, perhaps I'm obligated to answer the question. After all, I left the house. Let's see. Why did I adopt? Let me look at my side of the family. There's the guy who still lives in the basement, the girl with that tattooed back, biker, boozer, dead tooth, too many cats, the guy who talks to his truck...Hmmmm.

Maybe I adopted because, genetically, my balls are full of poison. I hate myself enough; I don't want to watch a little version of me shit his pants.

Clearly, though I protest, I obviously protest too much. I tease my father, but am in so many ways a miniature version of him. Like my father, I have two basic emotions, rage and suppressed rage.

My father was born during the Depression, and, like many working-class men who came of age in the segregated world of midcentury America, he is, by today's standards, often viewed as intemperate and racist.

That said, many of his accusers aren't white.

To my father's credit, he does not restrict his bigotry to the big three or four. He spreads it around. Often, you can hear him in the other room, watching the news, coming up with racial hatreds you didn't know were racial hatreds. I can hear him now, his voice thundering through our half of the duplex, "Oh, Jesus. There go the Belgians again. They're worse than the Burmese. The Belgians are just like Burmese with hangovers."

Do I approve? Heavens no. Have I ever brought it up? Heavens, heavens no. You see, the Goulds are not a close-knit group. Our family crest shows five lions watching television not speaking to each other, with MOVE YOUR HEAD written on a banner in Latin.

But now I have kids, and as I've gotten a taste of what my parents were up against, it has made it much more difficult to blame my mom and dad for everything negative that's ever happened to me. That's a shame, too, because it came in so handy. When I was in my twenties, I'd go to a party, not get laid, and blame my parents. It certainly couldn't be my fault—just because I talk too loud, don't go to the gym, and am built like a condom full of walnuts. "Thanks a lot, Dad."

My parents had six kids, back to back, with no additional help, and I was surprised they enjoyed a drink now and then. I have two kids, a nanny, and a housekeeper, and I'm about as relaxed as a hummingbird on a coke binge.

The fact of the matter is, my parents did the best they could.

There is no way to explain to people the seismic changes your life undergoes when you become a parent, from your daily schedule to your perspective on the world. In my case, it has totally ruined porn. Now I watch a movie with a nice girl and two or three guys, and all I think is, *Oh, Jesus, did her parents screw up.*

I have started seeing people not just as people, but as other people's children. And when I sneak quietly into the curtained back room of my local video store, all I can think is *Look at all these DVDs, starring someone's daughter!!! And look! Someone else's daughter! Look at this blazing someone's-daughter on someone-else's-daughter action!*

No thanks. "I've changed," I mutter, as I rent a nice comedy with Dennis Quaid that I won't watch and will return late. Welcome to the world of new perspectives and compromise.

Lots and lots of compromise.

We got our kids baptized into the Catholic faith. Not that I believe in it. I can't see how a medieval water-based ritual can affect a child's existential guilt. My parents believe in it. And my wife's parents believe in it. So off we went. I stood by smiling as a strange old man in a King Arthur costume dunked my daughter's head into a bucket, ensuring to the universe that when she died, she would be allowed to live atop a cloud in an invisible castle.

We felt pretty good about our decision to go along. Our parents were happy, and let's be honest, somewhere in the back of our minds we did think, *What if they're right? What if there is a God and He's exactly as described? He created you, He loves you, and He's created a world of molten agony to eternally punish you if you cross Him.*

Seriously. Just because I can't conceive of a thing does not mean it can't exist. My dog can't conceive of my computer, but they're both real. "Let's just go ahead and play it safe," we said to each other. "If there is a God, and these are His rules, then you know He's going to be a dick about enforcing them."

Now granted, some things are just too impossible to swallow. I mean, I can still take a stand when I have to. For instance, when I was a child, I was taught, by adults, that when I died, I had to stand in front of all of my relatives who were in heaven and say out loud all of the terrible things I had ever thought and done.

Thought?

I can assure you, that is not true. If anything, I believe that when I die, I will have to stand in front of all the children who went to bed hungry while I was on earth and read aloud a list of my eBay purchases. I shudder to think of it. Explaining to a poor child with a swollen belly why I didn't give his village fifty cents a week but spent twenty-seven dollars in a bidding war for a *Mars Attacks* coffee cup.

Next week. Next week I'm signing up for that feed-a-village thing. I promise. Like my parents before me... I'm doing the best I can.

HAVE I GOT A TRIP FOR YOU

Merrin Dungey

HAVING A BABY IS LIKE being offered a trip to Neptune. People you know have gone, and they say, "It's great, there's nothing like it, everyone should go!"

So you plan your trip and book it with the travel agent.

When you ask what it's like after you go to Neptune, she won't give you a straight answer. The fact is, though, everyone you know who has gone to Neptune is just *different* now. They are changed and can't explain all the reasons why. But you think, that won't happen to me, what could happen, I'll still be the same person, right? I mean, *really*, how different could my life be?

So the time comes, and you and your partner get in the rocket ship and go. For some people the trip is really amazing and easy and fast, and for some it's awful and they puke the whole entire time, and others have a really long, beautiful experience. And when you get back, all you can do is talk about the trip at first. That's all anyone who knows you wants to talk about anyway. Then, about three weeks later, you realize how different you are. How your life will never be the same. The things you've had to give up, the things you now are asked to do. Sometimes you catch a glimpse of yourself in the mirror and you can see your old self in there, but just slightly, oops, wait, shit, now it's gone. You'll hear a song on the radio and remember a time before going to Neptune when that song meant it's *the weekend* and you *can't wait* for so-and-so's party, or having a martini after work with friends, or that trip to *Vegas* that was off the hook. But now you've been to Neptune, and you only hear that song in the car rushing to the supermarket. Or you'll look in your closet and you can't *believe* you once wore a skirt that small, or that short, or heels that high, or that *expensive*. What were you thinking? Didn't you realize that you were going to Neptune someday and all those things would become utterly useless? Where are you going in $745 red suede Christian Louboutins now? And now that you've gone to Neptune, do they even fit?

It's so much easier to talk to those who have also traveled to Neptune. They walk around in the same fog that you do. They speak the same foreign tongue: "Onesie, binky, episiotomy, tummy time." They understand when you have to rush off to "pump" or deal with your "sleep schedule." They empathize about the witching hour and colic or your desperation to have time to watch *Project Runway*. They understand that TiVo is your lifeline to the outside world. They know. They, too, have been to Neptune—and know you can never go home again.

Now that I've been, I have a few things to say: I want to start by apologizing to my vagina. I just... I just didn't know what was going to happen. I thought it might be easy, or, well, easier than it was. All my life I've been told I have "child-birthing hips." Which turned out to be just a lie, a dirty goddamned lie. I pushed for three hours, and I put you, dear vagina, through hell, and I'm sorry. I just wish I could go back in time and get to know you better and appreciate your work more. I just... I just didn't know. I appreciate all your hard work and effort, and I know you tried. I tried to protect you. I did my best, and I'm really, really sorry. I can only hope that someday soon the bad feelings between us can be healed. I really hope that happens soon. This relationship has gotten really painful, and honestly, it's been weeks now. Please let the healing begin.

I would also like to apologize to my husband for many things. The inappropriate name-calling in the delivery room. All the resentment I had toward you because I had to carry her for nine months and you did not. And the name-calling I did then as well. I will have sex with you again someday. I promise, that will happen. I mean, don't hold your breath or anything, but we'll get there. I will wear attractive lingerie again as well. These grandma underpants aren't *forever*! Um...about my boobs. While I appreciate your attempts to touch them, I hope you understand that these are not for you at this time. These are working breasts, and they are under construction at the moment, and we appreciate your patience. It's funny; I can see both fear and delight in your eyes at the size of them. And trust me, they are something to fear. I never thought one boob could dwarf the size of my baby's head, but it's true. Her bravery to attack it day after day, literally head-on, is impressive. I must apologize to her as well. I had no idea that my boobs would operate in a sprinkler fashion when it came to feeding, and I have shot her in the face many, many, many times. My apologies there. But the way she fights back through the spray, which is a force to be reckoned with, is quite something. She is a brave, strong gal.

I apologize to any woman whose baby shower I attended before I had a baby. I just didn't know what you really needed, and all those useless stuffed animals and baby booties . . . well, I'm sure they came in handy at some point. I just should have stuck to the registry and got you some things you could have used right away. So sorry.

I need to quickly apologize to my cats for bringing home the "new hairless cat that gets all the attention these days." I'm sorry you can no longer sleep on the bed, and you have let me know how you feel about that with your poo. Message received.

I apologize once again to my husband, this time for criticizing you every time you dress our daughter. I know that she is my very own personal doll come to life, and I like to play dress-up, but you make such weird choices. Why would you put her in a sweater in August? It's the middle of the day—a nightgown, really? It's bedtime, sweetheart, why is she wearing a hat? I am going to try to hold my tongue; I recognize this is not *America's Top Model*, but I do ask you to just think about what makes sense sometimes, that's all.

I apologize to every mother I saw before I had a baby for judging your appearance. I mentally criticized those old sweatpants, big T-shirts, and haphazard ponytails. I thought you just hadn't taken the time to get ready before you went out, or you were in need of a makeover. Now I understand that you had simply fallen into that "mom thing." Perhaps we should get you on one of those special *Oprah* episodes. I am sorry because I was mean and misunderstood you, and I get it now. I understand those precious minutes that are savored when the baby goes down for a nap, the desperation to stretch them out, make the most of every minute. I could shower! I could eat! I could sleep! E-mail! Work out! Do laundry! Have sex! (Well, maybe not just yet, but . . .) I could do so much if she would just sleep for a few more minutes! And inevitably, there's that sound through the monitor. [Stop. Wait. Listen] . . . Was it for real? . . . That was just a sneeze, right? . . . Is she up? . . . She's not up, right? . . . Oh, please, I'm almost done, I'm almost done eating, the coffee's almost ready, I thought I could shower, just five more just five more minutes please just . . . *nope*. Fuck. She's up. She's hungry. She's wet. She's something. And once you've got her set, fed, watered, and changed, there you are, now on the clock to get that errand done before it all unravels again. There is absolutely no time for a blowout or blusher. I get it. I was a complete bitch, and I'm sorry. I'm really sorry because I see how people look at me now in the market, with that mixture of pity and disgust, in my old Old Navy nursing tank covered in spit-up and the same maternity shorts that I wear every goddamned day. I am like the elephant man. I put my daughter in fancy clothes when we go out, to compensate for the monster that is pushing her around. I see the stares, I know what you're saying. Well, fuck you, you small-pants-wearing Miley-Cyrus-loving fuckhead. I just had a baby. I am not always this fat. And I used to be on TV. Fuck you.

I guess I should also apologize for my anger. But in solidarity to new mothers everywhere I am *not* going to.

Finally, I'd like to apologize to my former self. I always thought you had a few pounds to lose and maybe you could look better. I never knew how good you had it, and I am really sorry. What I would give to fit into your clothes again! I look at you

longingly, day after day. Hi, jeans. Hello, Diane von Fursten-
burg wrap dress. You were all so good to me. Sigh. Good times.

I never appreciated my boobs enough. They were great boobs,
too, not too big, just enough décolletage. I mean, a really solid
couple of gals. They got the job done. And now...sigh...who
knows what will be left.

I should have slept in more. I used to beat myself up if I slept
past eight, or stayed out too late. I was a fool. A *fool*. What did I
know?

Oh, to do anything at all at a leisurely pace—shop, eat, read
the newspaper—and *anything* without having to wear a monitor
like a tricorder out of *Star Trek*. Waiting. Listening. For her. I'm
sorry, former self. I truly am.

One thing I will never be sorry about is that I took that trip
to Neptune. I don't know if I'll go again, but I know it was
worth it no matter how much it cost me. I can't really explain
it. You wouldn't understand. Not unless you've been.

MOM REDEFINED

Moon Unit Zappa

I THOUGHT I HAD OUTGROWN complaining about what I did and didn't get from my mom and dad when I got married (there's something about a husband and a mortgage that really lets you know you've come into your own). It wasn't until I had a kid that I began to suspect I might have to revisit my childhood and consider its potential impact on my own parenting.

Growing up the daughter of a sixties rock icon was pretty much what you might imagine: I called my parents by their first names, was offered a diaphragm at age twelve, and was told that when I had sleepovers I had to shower with whomever I was dating so we could save water. No energy was wasted on sheltering me from the big bad world; my three siblings and I knew the drill—our rock royalty of a dad toured for nine months out of the year, cheated on my mom when he was away, but always came back to us, to sleep all day and work all night. Growing up like this, my plan was to have a bunch of kids and raise them without a man around (just like my foxy, worldly mom, Gail), but my brood would be sired by a bunch of different dads, because I would sleep around too (just like my ultra-cool workaholic dad, Frank).

When I was little, "Mom" meant let people be themselves so Dad doesn't leave us for a groupie and we can keep food on the table and a roof over our heads. "Mom" meant do your own thing, because my mom didn't have time to play with us or teach us conflict resolution—she was too busy making sure my dad didn't leave us for a groupie. "Mom" meant yell a lot to get us to stop screaming so Dad can sleep so he can work and doesn't leave us for a groupie.

I remember other things too, like how Gail used to sweep her flaxen hair up in one motion using only a toothbrush to hold it in place. And the animated voices she'd use to make bedtime stories about vorpal blades and tar babies come alive when she read aloud to us from the "Jabberwocky" or Uncle Remus. She sewed all our Halloween costumes from scratch and transformed kitchen countertops into go-go stages. She let the cats lick the butter and still made us cinnamon toast with the slippery stuff. She went everywhere barefoot, even drove that way, and kept her figure doing side bends by our pool in the afternoon sun. I adored watching Gail apply mascara in her grown-up bathroom, the smell of my mom's hair detangler and her perfume and her pale skin. She was the loveliest woman I had ever seen.

Since my dad didn't drive, sometimes Gail would wake us in the middle of a school night, pile us into the back of the

Rolls-Royce without our seatbelts fastened, to pick Frank up from rehearsal. Then we'd hit an all-night taco stand to get my father a double order of red and green burritos. Many times we'd get lucky and Gail would be too tired to drive us to school the next morning, so we'd get to stay home all day, lying around on the family waterbed, watching as much TV as we wanted. Sometimes we'd get a turn making espresso for dad or sprinkling cayenne pepper on his afternoon scrambled eggs. Or even better, we'd win the coveted task of delivering my father's breakfast and a fresh packet of Winstons to him on a bamboo tray; I still recall the thrill of tiptoeing into the musky darkness of my father's bedroom and setting the tray down beside his naked, sleeping form.

My siblings and I spent many happy afternoons playing unsupervised in dogshit-encrusted ivy, fooling around with Ouija boards, trying to bend spoons with our minds and practicing our burgeoning ESP. We'd make prank calls on our rotary phones or draw on the walls with Sharpies or figure out alternate uses for handheld back massagers in the privacy of our bedrooms.

As I got a little older, "Mom" was also starting to mean too overwhelmed to pay close enough attention. Or be patient or kind. It meant no time for herself, no time to sleep, and then one day "Mom" meant tolerance for the unthinkable, like the time my dad moved a groupie into the basement for several weeks and we watched Gail put up with it so we could remain a family when I wished they'd get a divorce instead. Clearly "Mom" also meant resolve because Gail weathered that insane storm; eventually the outsider went home and normal life resumed.

Whenever I'd go to someone else's house to play, I'd observe alien behaviors, like moms and dads who stopped what they were doing and looked worried when their children were sad or hurt. Grown-ups who defended their kids when they were bullied, who offered comfort when their kids were frightened or angry or confused. These parents spent time with their kids, protected and effectively consoled them. Sure, these strange humans set boundaries and disciplined their kids (actions my family found reprehensible), but these people got along. Even more bizarre, soup and greater attention were offered to children when they were sick! In my house sick was shorthand for "push past it," "get it yourself," and "goddamnit, stop having needs!" Of course these foreign people were deadly dull, but at least they looked out for one another.

When I was fifteen, I developed chronic cystic acne and a suicidal depression I thought no one noticed. But then I remember Gail coming into my room one afternoon with a strange look on her face and handing me a parcel. The previously opened box was from Germany. It contained an extensive all-natural skin care line. I was confused and touched and sickened; my dad must have told the latest whore he was fucking overseas I had a case of crap skin. Though I desperately needed it, I promptly threw it all out when my mom wasn't looking.

By the time I was ready to leave home, the definition of "Mom" had expanded to include unfair rule through financial bondage, control through psychological and emotional manipulation, and profound apathy. On my eighteenth birthday it became clear I needed outside guidance, a.k.a. therapy.

In discreet nautical-themed offices around the city, I cried oceans spilling my guts, telling family secrets, and mourning childhood losses. I was informed I was raised by errant children unwittingly parenting as my absentee "adult" friends. How else do you explain celebrating my father on Mother's Day because he had a band called the Mothers of Invention? And, my God, my own flesh-and-blood parents never wanted us to call them Mom and Dad!

Over the next twenty years, in fifty-minute overpriced increments, I pondered my free-love upbringing and subsequent superdeluxe father complex, guessing at the hand-me-down damage of my family tree. After years of analysis and incalculable experimentations re-creating unfulfilling, well, *everything*, I sorted it all out. One thing was sure—my laissez-faire parents fucked my shit up. I vowed to anyone who would listen I would be the *opposite* of them; I was going to be a loving, patient, present, hands-on *mom*. Early one spring, at long last, I met a good guy, had a baby, and lived happily ever after.

Or so I thought.

Leave it to me to find the one musician in the world who wants to stay faithful and change his touring schedule around so he can participate in our child's life (a totally foreign concept to me) and *then* go on to give birth to a relentlessly independent daughter who could care less about my bottomless pit of codependent needs.

I would hear my husband cheerfully offering to change a poopy diaper or offering to let me sleep in and think, *Fuck you. Why don't you just go back to your studio and make music day and night just like my father did?* When my husband would start to rub my feet or make me a cup of tea, I'd think, *What? Fucking groupie whores isn't good enough for you?* Then he'd offer to take the baby for a few hours so I could have some time to myself and I'd think, *Why do you have to be such an asshole? Why can't you disappear for months on end like a normal daddy?*

When my daughter rejects the three meals I have prepared for her, and hasn't willingly hugged me in just as many days, when she erupts in squeals of delight just hearing the babysitter's car pull up the driveway, or protests teeth brushing, sleeping, and everything else I say or do like I'm some kind of death squad general, I can't help but think about my mom and dad, Gail and Frank, trying to raise my willful, mutant ass (along with my three siblings!).

With unflinching self-reflection I have learned to let my husband help me and to appreciate my daughter's autonomy. As I mother my child, I embrace the privilege of getting to re-mother myself; giving my child comfort when she's sad or helping her process her frustration feels like I'm stitching up the wounds of my unmet childhood needs.

Amen.

And yet, despite the fact that as a grown-up, I now define "Mom" to mean talking less and listening more, asking questions and slowing down, to mean appreciating process more than results, and having empathy for myself first so I can genuinely give the same to my child, despite all these ways I am trying desperately to do the job differently than my parents, I cannot claim with any certainty that I am doing it any better.

FAMILY VACATION
Kell Cahoon

IT'S OUR OLDEST SON'S FIRST vacation. We're headed to Family
Club Med Ixtapa, an all-inclusive resort on the fabulous
Mexican Riviera. As we pack the night before the trip, my wife,
Debbie, is a little nervous about going to Mexico with a six-
month-old baby. I'm more nervous about who we're going with.

Before I go on, let me be clear about something. I love my
wife's family. When I'm done, some of you *may* have the
impression that I find them obnoxious, annoying, intrusive,
irresponsible, ridiculous, buffoonish, drug-addled, and borderline insane. While technically this is true, they're also
some of the warmest, kindest, most fun-loving people you'd
ever want to meet.

The next morning, we arrive at LAX and it's a madhouse.

A long line of people is waiting to check bags, but since we've given ourselves plenty of time before our flight leaves, we aren't the least bit concerned.

While we wait on line, we pass the time holding hands and staring at our beautiful, chubby little boy. We are, as they say, one happy little family. We reach the front of the line and hand our tickets to the agent. She asks for our passports, which Debbie cheerfully retrieves from her bag. Then the agent asks for the baby's *birth certificate*.

And we are happy no more.

"I didn't know we had to bring a birth certificate," Debbie says, her normally husky voice rising several octaves. The agent explains that it's for our own protection and we can't get on the plane without it.

I'm focused on Debbie's face. She's getting a look I know all too well. Using Homeland Security's Color Advisory System, it's the equivalent of a Yellow (Elevated) Threat Level.

Finally, Debbie explodes. "Goddamnit! This is all my fault! I cannot wait to tell my parents they don't get to see their grandson because his mother is such a fuckup!"

I want to tell Debbie that it's no big deal. That, as usual, she's being too hard on herself. And that maybe she should try to avoid cursing, you know, in front of the baby. But I don't have the chance, because by now Debbie is punching herself in the forehead. Hard. The baby sees this and naturally starts to scream. People in line look horrified. I try to calm Debbie down by asking her to "bring down the hysterics a bit." In retrospect this wasn't the best choice of words. Kind of like poking a really emotional bear.

Luckily, the ticket agent assures us we'll have no trouble getting on the same flight the next day. Debbie eventually calms down after doing some deep breathing yoga exercises and slamming back a Bloody Mary in the airport bar.

The next morning we arrive back at the airport. As stressful as the previous day was, this day is as smooth as can be. The flight to Mexico City is a pleasure. Lucas sleeps the whole time. Debbie and I get to read, a rare treat. Even the in-flight chicken enchiladas are surprisingly tasty.

This vacation is starting to look up.

We reach the resort around noon. It's a hot, humid day, and because our taxi's "air-conditioning" is just a battery-operated personal fan taped to the dashboard, the three of us are sweating buckets. Debbie's family is waiting for us at the hotel entrance, looking all tanned and relaxed.

My mother-in-law, Beverly, and Debbie's sister, Shari, get into a shoving match as they try to be the first one to hold the baby. My father-in-law, Al, gives me a big hug and says, "I know your people are uncomfortable with public affection, but too bad 'cuz you're gonna get kissed!" With that, he plants a big one right on my lips.

I'm standing there, the taste of Marlboro Lights lingering in my mouth like an obnoxious, uninvited party guest, and I want to scream, while spitting, "You're damn right I'm uncomfortable with it! Especially that kind, you lunatic!"

Instead, I just smile. See, I was raised to believe that the worst thing a person can do is to make a scene. No matter how uncomfortable or angry or humiliated someone makes you feel, for God's sake keep it hidden. This is known as "the WASP Way," and other than giving me chronic stomach pain and a tendency to abuse alcohol, it has served me pretty darn well so far.

At this point, my brother-in-law, Mike, pulls me aside. Mike's a successful CPA in New York. He's obsessed with numbers, both in his work and his leisure time. Which is why he's eager to show me the plastic yellow wristband he purchased at the resort bar. "It cost me $175 and gets me all I can drink for the week," he says. "So far today, I've had three Bloody Marys, six beers, and a piña colada. At the rate I'm going, I should break even around noon tomorrow. After that, I'm drinking for free, baby!"

"Wow, that's great, Mike," I say.

"I'll keep you posted on how it's going," he replies.

"Yeah, please do."

We all head inside, where I check in at the front desk and get our keys. Now, whenever we arrive at a hotel, Debbie insists on unpacking the second we're in the room. She can't relax until she's divvied up the drawers, neatly put away our clothes, and carefully arranged the toiletries in the bathroom. This process normally takes from three to four hours.

But I'm anxious to officially start the vacation. Even though I know the answer will be no, I find myself asking—okay, more like begging—"Please, just this once, let's throw caution to the wind, drop off the bags, change quickly into our bathing suits, and head straight for the pool, what do you say?" To my utter amazement, Debbie says okay.

Has the earth just shifted on its axis? Has my cute little control freak of a wife finally thrown off the shackles of her rigid inflexibility and learned to go with the flow?

When we get to our room, I find out the truth behind Debbie's new devil-may-care attitude. She's neglected to tell me we're sharing connecting rooms with her parents. Under normal circumstances, this would not be that big a deal, but, as I've said, Debbie's family is not normal. They have boundary issues. As in they have none. For example, there was the time my father-in-law invited me for a chat in the stairwell outside their apartment in New York—the only place where Bev lets him smoke. Now, it's not that I'm some stickler about breathing secondhand smoke, but couldn't the man have at least put on pants? I stood there for an hour while Al dissected the New York Yankees season wearing nothing but a gold neck chain and a pair of tighty whities. It is an image that is forever burned in my brain.

Debbie sees I'm not happy with the connecting rooms situation, but she assures me the positives outweigh the negatives. "Honey, this way, my parents can help with the baby whenever we need them to. And they said they'll babysit one night so we can go out to dinner."

"Gee, no offense, hon, but I'm not really comfortable leaving our precious baby with your folks just yet," I say.

Debbie adds, "And after dinner, you might even get lucky."

"However, you make an excellent point, it is more convenient this way—and hey, we get to skip unpacking and go straight to the pool so what the heck I'm sure Lucas will be fine with your parents last one in their bathingsuitisarottenegg!"

When Debbie and I stroll Lucas up to the pool area some twenty minutes later, my father-in-law is trying to take a picture of Debbie's nephews, Max and Matt, ages five and seven. Max and Matt are acting like typical uncooperative boys and refusing to smile. This so infuriates their grandfather that he yells for all to hear, "Keep it up, you retards, and I'm cutting you out of the will!"

My mother-in-law quickly steps in. "Leave it to me, Al. I know how to get them to smile." She proceeds to grab her very large boobs, juggle them, and sing out, "C'mon, boys, look at Grandma's Jell-O!"

It works. Matt and Max burst out laughing. Al takes the picture. "Great job, Bev. That's a winner!"

I have just witnessed my son's grandmother shaking her tits. I decide now would be a good time for a stiff drink. Maybe two. I start for the bar.

Bev sees me. "Where you going, honey?" she asks.

"Oh, just to get a drink."

"Let Mike get it. He's got the wristband." She calls to Mike, who's walking toward us. "Mike, get Kell a drink."

"That's okay, I don't mind paying for it," I say.

Now Al chimes in. "Don't be an idiot. Why should you pay? That's why Mike's got the wristband. Mike, get Kell a drink."

I say, okay, fine, I'll take a frozen margarita.

Mike nods. "You got it." Only he doesn't move. He stays put.

"With salt," I say, in case that's why he's waiting.

Mike looks around, then leans over and whispers, "Okay, here's the deal. I just got a strawberry daiquiri, and the rules are I can only get drinks for myself. So just sit tight, I'll go back in a few and get the margarita. Then meet me over by the bathrooms and I'll make the handoff."

I'm thinking, *I just want a drink, not the microfilm for some supersecret Nazi submarine.* But as I said, I was not raised to make waves. So I go along with Mike's plan.

A few minutes turn into twenty. Then an hour. Then two. The sun beats down on me like an angry Mexican ball of fire. I'm dying of thirst. Mike and his sons are busy playing in the pool, and I can't bring myself to butt into their fun and ask, "Hey, what ever happened to that margarita?"

And every time I start to get up from my chair, my in-laws want to make sure it's not to sneak off to pay for my own drink, because Mike's got the wristband. So I'm forced to sit in the boiling sun as my throat turns into sandpaper and think about how I have to spend *six* more days with these people.

Here are a few highlights from the week:

DAY 2. I pull a calf muscle playing in the tennis tournament. I fall to the ground, writhing in pain. Al is watching in the bleachers and yells at me to "walk it off!" I have to forfeit the match because I can't walk, and I hear Al tell the lady next to him that I'm a "big pussy."

DAY 3. It's Al and Bev's night to babysit. When I go next door to get them, their room is filled with smoke. Pot smoke. They're lying in bed and puffing on a fattie. Naturally I react, pissed off. My father-in-law scoffs, "Please, we're not so high we can't take care of one little baby."

DAY 5. Mike is competing in the Annual Ocean Swim Race. He starts off the race looking good, especially for a guy who had a mai tai with breakfast. The family and I cheer him on from the beach.

Halfway through the race, as he makes the turn and heads for home, Mike starts to gasp for air. He struggles to stay above water. My sister-in-law screams, "Oh my God, Mike's drowning!" My nephews burst into tears and cry out, "Please, Daddy, don't die!"

We yell for a lifeguard. What a surprise, there isn't one. So I hop down to the surf. Mike manages to reach the shallow water, and I drag him the rest of the way in. I'm about to give him mouth-to-mouth when, thankfully, he starts to vomit. Every color in the spectrum seems to gush forth from him. It's like some tropical-themed fountain you'd see at a Vegas hotel.

Later, at the bar, the family laughs and celebrates how great it is that Mike isn't dead. Mike says he's sure learned his lesson about mixing sports and booze as he gulps down his third sea breeze.

I can't seem to join in on the fun. There's this nagging voice in my head that keeps saying, "Are these people completely divorced from reality?!"

It's at this point, steeped in my own sense of superiority and righteousness, that I notice something.

My son, Lucas, six months old, is having the time of his life. He is being doted on, cuddled, kissed, spoiled, and loved. These ridiculous people are absolutely crazy about him. And he can't get enough of them.

I realize that when you have children, you go on family vacations. And family vacations are not the same thing as vacations. They're something completely separate and distinct. They have nothing to do with you. They're for the kids. So I decide to stop passing judgment and jump into this family with both feet. I start for the bar to get a drink.

My mother-in-law sees me. "Where are you going, honey?"

"To get a drink."

"Let Mike get it. Mike, get Kell a drink."

Mike looks around, leans over, and whispers, "Okay, here's the thing..."

HERE COMES THE SON

Mimi Friedman

I WAS VERY SHAKY ON the decision to become a parent. I mean, I was already in my late forties, and terrified to give up whatever it was I did then. I went to movies whenever I wanted, ate at great restaurants almost every night, spent hours at Book Soup, Urth Caffé, Burke Williams, traveled to wherever, whenever—no wonder I was terrified. But what I was terrified of most was giving up my undivided attention to myself. With a child, there'd be no more spacing out in the garden hammock. No more mindlessly watching klieg lights sweeping the Hollywood sky for the premiere of a new Toyota dealership. No more watching police helicopters circling the neighborhood with a high-powered spotlight hoping to capture an armed fugitive crouching in a clump of ficus. No more of those meditative transcendent moments for me.

My mother always told me I'd make a great mother, but I silently dismissed the possibility because I knew I was gay from an early age. Back then, Anita Bryant advertised orange juice. The former Miss America's big toothy smile and hateful agenda seeped into my consciousness along with every other signal from society that completely squelched the idea that motherhood could be in any part of my future.

Well, now my partner and I have a son, and where exactly is Anita? Probably safely tucked away in some gated community preparing picnic baskets for the Rapture.

I didn't want to adopt, but what with my hysterectomy, pregnancy would be a little tricky. My partner had decided after a lot of soul searching that adoption was the way to go. God, "partner" is such a cold word. I know Melissa Etheridge says "wife," but it's just not for me.

When we were doing the final legal adoption in front of the judge at Family Court, he asked how long we had been "friends." The great State of California granted us the right to adopt as a couple, but apparently we were just "friends." "Hey, 'friend'! Want to go shopping, have lunch, then maybe adopt a child or two?" I guess the court hasn't found the right word either.

Open adoption. We'd be face-to-face with a birth mother who would be giving up her child to us. I had no frame of reference for this. It was more terrifying than the thought of losing all my idle shopping time.

My oldest sister was adopted, and she was passed off by a third party to my parents. That was that. No direct contact. That sounded pretty good to me. When adoption came seriously into the picture, I also became acutely aware of a fairly hideous bias of mine. I was Jewcentric.

My adopted sister was raised by the same parents in the same house since she was two days old, but she was different from the rest of us. She loved white bread and canned cream-style corn and bad boys, and her waist was the size of most of the women in my family's wrists. Just different. I started to think of it as cultural DNA. Somehow, Jews carried the memory of five thousand years of experience that made them fully appreciate Larry David and not only tolerate but delight in gefilte fish. Okay, so my sister loved gefilte fish and my Jewish girlfriend hated it. "Girlfriend?" Also, so wrong. I began to obsess. Cultural DNA is powerful. It's something that could create a shorthand of understanding with my child, a more subtle level of communication. If we adopted, that couldn't happen.

I asked our lawyer if any Jewish babies ever came up for adoption. Never. Jews would probably overcook and eat their young before they'd give them up. He recommended that we run ads in the classifieds of *Soap Opera Digest* as part of our search for a birth mother. My God. All I could think of was some young girl knocked up in the Midwest hooked on cough syrup and *All My Children*. Who would her kid turn out to be? Could a child escape its origins? Wait a minute. What was I thinking? I was so disgusted with myself. Although it's the reverse of the Nazi/Aryan ideology, it's the same thing. "Could a child escape its origins?" That could easily have been pillow talk between Hitler and Eva Braun.

Thank God my spouse was more openhearted. "Spouse?" Not *so* terrible. So we proceeded. The lawyer told us we had to write a letter to the potential birth mothers describing ourselves, so they could use it as a guide in making their choice. He told us to use the simplest language and decorate the letter colorfully—and include photos. It ended up looking and reading like a second-grade book report on our lives. "We love music and dogs and all our friends and family and trees, and cupcakes, sunshine, lollipops, and rainbows!" We included every photo we had of either one of us and any child we knew. Our book report could have been titled *"The Happy-Go-Lucky but Stable Lesbians of Ogden Drive,* by Beverly Cleary."

He then suggested we compose three versions of the letter: one as a couple and the other two as single mothers in case a birth mother was homophobic. As I wrote my fake single-woman version, I started to feel unsettled and a little sad. I mean, how lame that we were having to do this little charade to make us more palatable. And I really didn't like the thought of bringing a baby into our house from deceptive beginnings. Still, we handed in all three versions of ourselves and waited. Not quite a week later, we got a call. "You've been chosen." I asked what version the birth mother had read, and he said, "None." He told us that he had started to describe us and she stopped him almost immediately. "They are the ones. I just feel it," she had said.

There was a phone call set up for the three of us. She had an easy laugh and cut to the chase. "I want to ask you a question." My heart jumped. What would she ask? Were we good Christians? Were we truly committed to each other? She said, "Do you want to be at the birth?" She was the one.

She was eight and a half months pregnant, presently single, had two young girls of her own.

We were to meet her at her ob-gyn appointment. We got there first, and no one else was in the waiting room. We looked at the sign-in sheet. No, she wasn't there yet. I felt dizzy as I stared at a picture of Katie Couric on the cover of *Ladies' Home Journal.* Katie had two biological kids. She didn't have to go through this. Suddenly, the door flew open and in she waltzed. She didn't look at us but walked directly to the sign-in sheet. Her manner was light and breezy. "Hello, lovely ladies!" I tried not to size up her physical traits, but I couldn't help it. She was tall and had a thick braid of blond hair. Great hair! Her white overalls were stretched where her belly protruded, but otherwise she didn't seem puffy or weighed down in any way. They called her in immediately, and she told us to come in with her. We waited in the hall as she got undressed and then called for us.

In we went to find her in the stirrups. Hi, nice to meet you and your uterus. The doctor came in and started to examine her. I backed up against the wall and wanted to push through it and disappear, but in the next few minutes, she made us feel like this was completely normal and just what had to be done. I looked at the ultrasound. There was a boy in there, and he was going to be our son. She told the doctor she didn't, under any circumstances, want a C-section. What if there were complications and she had to have a C-section? Absolutely not. No scars.

We walked her back to her car. We talked about nothing, but she was funny and had a naturalness that was appealing. We watched as she drove away, feeling a little relieved. As she rounded the parking lot, she waved good-bye, and we saw that she was holding a cigarette. How could she smoke during our pregnancy? What was she doing to our baby? We tried to rationalize that our mothers had smoked during their pregnancies and we turned out all right. Mostly. Still, it was tough to realize that we had no say in the matter. This was her body, and she could do whatever she felt like doing. My strong feelings about a woman's right to choose were being seriously challenged.

I spent a lot of the next two weeks at the Juvenile Shop sitting in slider rockers and staring at Diaper Genies. There's a reason nature provides a gestation period of nine months. This was happening way too fast. There were two more doctor's appointments with her. Then one day, as I was buying some overpriced Kiehl's baby products, I got the call that her water had broken. Amazingly, to get our baby, we didn't have to go across the country or overseas. We had to go over the hill. To the Valley. Tarzana/Encino Medical Center. We practically flew.

We were preparing for an all-nighter; she surprised us and delivered at the more civilized cocktail hour. Every time she screamed out in pain, my right foot would involuntarily slam down on the floor, as if it wanted to take on some of the work. But three big pushes and he was out. The doctor asked if I wanted to cut the cord. My hands were shaking, but I did it. She beamed as she held him tight. It was a look of pure love. We wanted to leave the room and give her that time, but she insisted that we hold him, too. I held him close and marveled at the tiny little Cary Grant cleft in his sweet chin. I recognized him. This was our boy. That cultural DNA thing dissolved into cultural DMA—Doesn't Mean Anything.

She stayed the night in the hospital, and we went home, well aware that she had twenty-four hours to change her mind. We got very little sleep. The next morning, we drove back to the hospital, exhilarated but anxious. We called her room to see if we could bring her breakfast. She said yes, so I immediately turned into the parking lot of Jerry's Deli. Then she said, "Don't worry."

She knew our fears and told us exactly what we needed to hear. I wanted to bring her everything on that ridiculously large menu.

When I entered her room, she was curled up in a ball and looked like a little girl. Someone had given her a stuffed teddy bear, and she was holding it. Her vulnerability was overwhelming. A while later we met her two girls, who had read to the baby throughout her pregnancy. They were sweet and loving, and I couldn't imagine what they understood about all this.

As we adored our son through the nursery window, she legally signed him away to us. A young woman who was in the room next to hers was also giving up her child for adoption, and was having a hard time. She went and talked to her. She helped her. Then she ate a turkey pastrami sandwich and a black-and-white cookie. Her counseling had been so effective, the lawyer offered her a job. She turned it down. It didn't pay nearly as much as her work, and she had mouths to feed.

Later that afternoon, as she braided her thick hair, her mother, a wiry woman with deep laugh lines, helped her prepare to leave. As they headed out, her mother turned to us and in a careful, measured tone said, "Take care of that boy." Without hesitation, her daughter responded, looking me right in the eyes, "I have no doubt." Then she hugged us both and walked out. Just like that. We were silent. After a moment, we started to cry and didn't stop for some time. We cried, because she couldn't.

Later, on that first night, I was frantically trying to find a tiny pair of plastic tongs that pulls the nipple through the plastic ring of the bottle. I had to find them. The baby needed those tongs to be happy and content and safe and loved and protected! All my fears completely focused on those damn tongs. When I found them, I suddenly thought of the birth mother. What was she feeling at that moment? Why did she do what she did? How could she do it? The reasons were hers alone. But I knew she understood what she gave us. And she was proud of that.

Sometimes, I see her face in his. It might seem odd, but I like it. Because if he has one ounce of the kind of grace that she does, he'll do okay.

Plus, the kid has great hair.

THE GAY STRAIGHT DAD

Mark Hudis

HERE'S MY DIRTY LITTLE SECRET: I'm the gayest straight man in America. If I didn't enjoy sex with women, I'd be living in a Greenwich Village walk-up with six cats, potpourri, and Jim J. Bullock.

At a bar, I order drinks with as many chunks of fruit, cherries, bendy-twisty straws, and mini umbrellas as they can cram into a frosted pink mug. Last year I dragged my poor wife to Stephen Sondheim's seventy-fifth birthday gala at the Hollywood Bowl; when Angela Lansbury stepped onstage, I gasped, my hand to my chest, and then joined in as 49,000 gay men sang along to *Sweeney Todd*. I'm proud to admit that although I haven't yet seen *Iron Man*, the new Indiana Jones flick, or *Speed*

Racer, I have seen *Sex and the City* twice and would be happy to go a third time if anyone is interested.

When I found out Natalya was pregnant, I did the least masculine thing possible: I wept, bought a dozen parenting books, curled up with some Sleepytime tea, and read about fatherhood. The books seemed thorough, but after being a dad for nearly a year and a half, I've realized something: Those books are written for real men. Manly men who use power saws and play through the pain and couldn't sing along with Doris Day belting out "I'm Not at All in Love" from the sound track of *The Pajama Game* if their life depended on it.

The books simply didn't prepare me for the three biggest challenges of fatherhood because those challenges are unique to overly emotional men, men like me who cry more easily than a roomful of premenstrual women watching mute orphans re-enact scenes from *The Notebook*.

OVERLY EMOTIONAL FATHER CHALLENGE NUMBER one: How to stop yourself from crying and/or exploding when your ten-month-old thinks you're a douche bag.

It was six in the morning. Joshy was awake, and even though I'd put him to bed only eleven hours earlier, I missed him. I was excited to start the morning daddy-style, with a big old toss in the air, the customary scraping of diarrhea off his balls, and, time permitting, some competitive peekaboo.

So I snuck up to his door, opened it just a crack, and peeked through to see him grinning from ear to ear and staring expectantly at the closed door. I threw it open and cheered, "Joshy!"

And he said, almost in tears, "No! No! Ma-ma! Ma-ma! Ma-ma! No!"

I kept smiling. "Joshy, it's me, Daddy!" I did a funny dance. I made funny faces. I gave him a little tickle.

And then he said, "No! No! Ma-ma, ma-ma, maaaaa-maaaaaa, ma (*gasp*) ma (*gasp*) ma (*gasp*) ma (*gasp*) . . ."

Now, real men, I'm told, would shrug this off, change the kid's diaper, and never give this massive rejection by an infant another thought. But I couldn't let it go. I'm too emotional. My mood swung from despondent to irritated and beyond, until I wanted to say to Josh, "Look, you little asshole, I pay for everything! That blankie you're using to dry your little baby tears? Mine. Mr. Hippo and the Barnyard of Joy? Mine. The calcium your body uses to build bones so you don't collapse like a soufflé was in the milk I bought for you! And I didn't buy the milk at Ralph's, I bought it at Whole Foods because I want only the best for my boy since you mean more to me than life itself, so when I come into your room I don't want crying and rejection, I want smiles and acceptance and peals of delighted fucking laughter, do you hear me?!"

I didn't actually say any of this, by the way.

OVERLY EMOTIONAL FATHER CHALLENGE NUMBER TWO: Maintaining inner peace despite a greatly increased number of accusations that I'm stupid from my lovely wife.

We all know trying to save your marriage by having a baby is like trying to ward off a heart attack by eating a crème-brûlée-filled cow. Luckily Natalya and I have a good marriage, and before we had a son, our fights were basically foreplay.

"You know, Mark, I'm the lucky one in our relationship!"

"No, Natalya, I'm the lucky one."

"No, I am."

"No, I am."

"No, I am, touch black no backs!"

"I am, touch your right boob!"

Then we'd have sex like teenagers. Lots of "not there's!" and a sprint to the finish.

But since we both have volatile tempers, when we do have a real fight it's a lot like the first twenty minutes of *Saving Private Ryan*. So before Josh was born, we only argued when there was really something to argue about. Natalya, knowing how emotional I am, would only bring up something if it *really* bothered her. But since Josh's arrival and the increased stress parenthood can bring, Natalya has lost a bit of her ability to shield me when I annoy her. For instance:

Natalya: "Mark, could you bring me Joshy's blue shoes?"

So I go to his room, grab the shoes, and bring them to Natalya.

Natalya: "I said his blue shoes."

Me: "Those are his blue shoes."

Natalya: "No, those are his teal slippers."

Me: "Oh, they look blue."

Natalya: "Only if you're color-blind. And they're not shoes, they're slippers."

Me: "What's the difference?"

Natalya: "The difference is, slippers are for walking inside, shoes are for walking outside."

Me: "Well, Josh doesn't walk anywhere, so technically he wears shoes for decoration and so the neighbors don't think we're poor. And by the way, they look like shoes."

Natalya: "Yes, they do look like shoes—if you're brain damaged."

Me: "Well, we know I'm brain damaged, because I married you."

Natalya: "Well, guess what, pal, you weren't my first choice!"

Me: "You whore!"

Natalya: "Suck my ass!"

This kind of argument would have been unthinkable before we had a baby. Not anymore. And it's my fault, because most real men, I'm told, would be secure enough to let an occasional prickly comment slide. But I can't. I feel every barb too deeply. So I fuel the fire and we can honestly wind up fighting about anything: Lawn care. *Top Chef.* Even something as mundane as telling time.

Me: "I think Joshy could use a nap."

Natalya: "He's only been up for two hours."

Me: "More like two and a half."

Natalya: "Um, no, he woke up at seven, and it's nine."

Me: "Um, he woke up at six forty-three. I had set my alarm for six forty-five, and when I heard him squeak I remember saying, 'Uch, I could've slept two more minutes.'"

Natalya: "Do you remember playing leapfrog with a unicorn? 'Cuz that never happened either. I woke up with Joshy at seven, and I know this because I flipped on the TV and the *Today* show was just starting."

Me: "Okay, you're delusional, and he woke up at six forty-three."

Natalya: "You have early onset Alzheimer's. Seven o'clock."

Me: "Six forty-three. You're getting fat."

Natalya: "Seven, which is twice as long as your dick, in inches."

Me: "How would you know, you haven't touched my dick in three months!"

Natalya: "Best three months of my life!"

Me: "Ice queen!"

Natalya: "Bald midget!"

OVERLY EMOTIONAL FATHER CHALLENGE NUMBER three: Getting used to the idea that the first year of your baby's life is a party for two, and you're not invited.

It's just that simple. Babies need their mommies. They need their warmth and their immunity and their milk and their touch and their love. All babies need from their fathers is twenty-three chromosomes and approximately sixty thousand dollars.

While Natalya was pregnant, I'd daydream about the future and in my mind's eye see us as a family of three skipping places, group hugging, rollin' up our pants legs and goin' down to the ol' fishin' hole, but most of all I pictured myself as a leader, a pillar of knowledge, strength, and comfort—like my dad was for me when I was little. That was my fantasy. Reality is different.

What I imagined: Joshy bumps his head. Natalya is traumatized, so I spring into action, scoop up the baby, and with a few deft moves have him laughing just seconds later. My wife looks on in loving admiration as our family bond is strengthened.

Reality: Josh bumps his head. Before Natalya can get to him, I scoop him up to prove what a great caregiver I am, hoist him onto my shoulders, and accidentally smack his head against the top of a door frame. He screams, Natalya takes him to the Grove, and I don't see either of them for six hours.

What I imagined: Joshy can't sleep. Natalya can't calm him. I stride in, say a few magic words, and he drifts off for twelve hours. Natalya is so turned on by my parenting skills we make love all night long.

Reality: Josh can't sleep. I can't calm him. Natalya strides in. I snap "I can do it!" Turns out I can't. Josh throws up. Natalya takes over. I skulk off to the den to masturbate.

I don't want any of this to come across as overwhelmingly negative. I'm so blessed it's almost embarrassing. I have a magnificent wife who's bright, funny, and gorgeous, a son who's a never-ending joy, and a home life that's wonderful. But I do tend to feel things more acutely than some people—both criticism and praise. I spent thirty days at the Betty Ford Center a few years ago to treat an addiction, and while I was there the medical staff explained that this is a common trait among addicts—a heightened sensitivity to everyday feelings. Before treatment it felt like a burden, but I've come to realize it's actually a blessing. It just means a life of higher highs and lower lows. And, sadly for Natalya and Joshy, it means having to endure spontaneous outbursts of "I got the horse right here, his name is Paul Revere." I hope they don't mind too much.

BEFORESKIN AND AFTER

Christy Callahan

I DON'T *REALLY* BELIEVE IN God. I use the qualifier "really" because I'm uncomfortable with the word "atheist"—it's aggressive and connotes some kind of activism or activity on my part. I mean, just because you like to walk around naked doesn't make you a "nudist." I grew up in a big Irish Catholic family near Boston. We went to church every Sunday, confessed our sins to priests through black screens, and gave up ice cream for Lent, and a few years ago, our parish priest was indicted for pedophilia—your typical Catholic childhood. I never felt connected to the Catholic Church unless it involved Christmas presents or Easter candy. Still, the official separation came after I got my driver's license and skipped Sunday school to go to the movies. A committed sinner, I lied to my mother about going to Mass well into my thirties.

When I entered the entertainment business after college and—sorry to employ an old stereotype—was surrounded by Jews, I knew I'd finally found my people! While dating my future Jewish husband, I agreed to raise our (as yet imaginary) children Jewish. Why not? I liked what I knew about the Jews: They live in big cities, they hate mayonnaise, they like movies, they're funny, there are *very* few in jail, and they call their parents every day. My kind of kids! Sign me up! My knowledge of the more religious rituals of Judaism was limited to the movie *Yentl* and a seder in college, which devolved into a big Manishevitz drinking game.

Years later, when I became pregnant with a boy, my husband, Jon, started talking about our son's "bris." "You mean a party when a baby gets his pee-pee snipped while people eat snacks? That's not happening!!" I said. "It's a *covenant*!" he shot back. "What the hell is a covenant?" I asked, imagining something to do with *Raiders of the Lost Ark*. "A covenant is a *thing*. A thing that Abraham agreed to with God. He was ninety-nine years old and got circumcised as a . . . covenant." "You think an image of an old man's uncircumcised penis is going to help?" A little background: Catholics do not recognize the existence of genitalia of any variety, *at all*, never mind celebrate it with bagels. The closest ceremony we have to a bris—a christening— involves a baby dressed in a gown made from of yards of diaphanous silk, camouflaging not only the genitalia but the *entire baby*.

Eventually, Jon declared the bris to be a "deal breaker," and I agreed, and not only because of my lack of religious conviction.

The reality was, an uncircumcised penis was as mythological to me as a unicorn or a Republican in West Hollywood. I'd heard tales about them, but I never considered them to be, you know—real. Even when my best girlfriend returned from a year in Paris reporting the details of her French boyfriend's foreskin with the gravitas of Sir Edmund Hillary describing a rare butterfly living atop Mount Everest, I was dubious. So, since I was okay with the circumcision part, I felt having a bris was a gift I could give Jon and his family.

Just an aside: It represents significant progress for Catholic girls everywhere that I can even type the words "uncircumcised penis" over and over, to be published under my own name and read by the public.

After my son, Cal, was born, Jon's entire family installed themselves in my hospital room and hashed out details of the upcoming bris: "Where will it be?" "What's his Hebrew name?" "What kind of food?" "What time works for Aunt Diane?" "You can't have it at your house—it's too messy." As the debate raged, I panicked. The foreskin was no longer theoretical—it belonged to my precious newborn, about whom I felt ferociously protective.

I *gently* pulled Jon aside. "What the *fuck*?" I asked. "What? You *knew* we were having a bris!" "I know," I said, "but let's just have it in the hospital. It will be safer, less stressful, and we won't have to hire a caterer." Jon replied, "Right, except we're having a bris."

I had no choice, so I laid down ground rules:

1. No nearsighted mohel doing shtick. ("Ten seconds to *tip* off!")
2. A doctor/mohel would do the operation.

3. The circumcision would take place in private, before the snacks.

I informed my family on the East Coast, and despite clear grounds for objection, they respectfully signed on and flew into town.

Eight days later, we decamped to our friends' large and exceptionally tidy house for the bris. I'd spent the previous week in contented isolation with my peaceful baby, my peaceful baby nurse, and my peaceful Vicodin. I was so mellow, I was practically Jamaican. The doctor/mohel arrived at the master bedroom/staging area, and I was stricken by how *happy* he was to be there. My mother, on the other hand, paced the room eying the baby as if she might abscond with him at any second. The mohel asked if I wanted to be present during the procedure.

"Of course!" I said.

"Well, most mothers leave the room," he warned.

"Not me, man, I'm okay."

We brought Cal into the closet, a room several times the size of an apartment I once lived in in New York—a labyrinth of clothes, shoes, and walls. I held my son tightly as we watched the mohel unpack a medieval torture device to immobilize the baby. Cal, like a Jedi Knight, sensed imminent danger and began to wail. I'd never heard him cry that way before, and instinctively I refused to let him go. Finally, out of an insecure desire not to be labeled "crazy mommy," I handed him over. My adrenaline surged as the mohel strapped Cal in, said some words in Hebrew, and put a drop of wine on his quivering lips. Cal's cries grew so loud the family beagle was howling outside the door. When the mohel went in with the scalpel, I freaked out and lunged to rescue my suffering baby—*That's right, crazy mommy's here, and you and Abraham's shriveled ninety-nine-year-old dick can kiss my ass.* Jon quickly scooped me up and "guided" me to the opposite end of the gargantuan closet. "Stay here. I'll be back in two minutes, it's almost over." Huddled behind a giant wall of shoes, I stuck my fingers in my ears and sang my default sound-covering tune, the *Facts of Life* theme song. It didn't work.

I looked around for a different distraction—a book! It was called *Four-Year-Olds: A Parent's Guide.* Now, if anything can terrify a new mother more than ritual circumcision, it's learning what's in store four years down the road. Page 29: "To express anger, a four-year-old will sometimes defecate on the floor." Really? After what felt like about seventeen more hours of sheer physical pain (on my part, and I assume Cal's), Jon returned, and I was allowed to pick up my son. After that, my memory becomes a bit hazy, but I know my mother and I stayed upstairs with Cal for a while (secretly agreeing that if I had another son, this would *not* be happening again), and Jon went downstairs to schmooze with the sixty guests waiting in the living room.

Before I started writing this, I dug up the pictures of Cal's bris, trying to remember the rituals of the ceremony, the words spoken, and people who were there. I mostly just remember the people. Several important ones are no longer with us: Jon's grandfather and grandmother and my own father. Because of their age, they held places of honor at the ceremony, and we have pictures of each one holding Cal, the first family member to be related to them all by blood. Even though my dad was Irish Catholic, he wore his yarmulke and read from the Torah with as much pride as if he were singing "Danny Boy."

Cal and his younger *sister*, Mae, now attend a Jewish nursery school, and after my father died, the not-really-an-atheist part of me struggled with telling them, "Papa Tom is in heaven," or, "He's with God." The rabbi said, "Jews don't believe that God is a person. That's a more Christian notion. God is family, God is tradition, and God is the bonds we form with our friends and community." I had never heard this before (and honestly, I'm not sure that the rabbi didn't make it up on the spot), but still it gave me comfort. When I look through the photographs of that day, and see the joy on the faces of the many friends and family with whom we've celebrated so many milestones, I think I might have found a version of an almighty power I can get behind.

SPOILED MILK

Johanna Stein

GOD, I'M GOOD AT THIS motherhood thing.

My daughter was born December 28, 2006. She was two weeks overdue, but who can blame her? She enjoyed being inside of me as much as I enjoyed having her there. Yeah, I'm one of those jerks who just loved being pregnant.

Even the delivery was a rockin' good time. After the epidural worked its rubber-legged magic I was joking and laughing, and then I squeezed out that eight-pound ten-ounce baby like I'd squeeze a watermelon seed through my fingers.

A few seconds after she was born, my kid grabbed right onto my nipple and nursed like she'd been doing it all her life. Which, if you do the math, she had been.

Even my recovery was pretty much trouble-free, right down

to that first poop. Mine, that is. They warn you that your first postdelivery poop will be excruciating, and when I felt the telltale abdominal rumblings on day three I trudged into the bathroom, squatted, and braced myself for tears, but the experience turned out to be downright pleasant. In fact, when it was over I felt renewed, as though my bumhole had been replaced, as though God himself had picked up the Grand Canyon, shaken it out like a damp towel, and let it settle, although this time the valleys had become peaks and the peaks valleys. I called it my brand-new anus, just another perk of the motherhood game—the game that I was clearly winning.

Until our one-week pediatrician appointment revealed that our perfect little girl had lost nearly 20 percent of her birth weight—double what was acceptable. Failure to thrive, he called it. Even though she was nursing every three hours, she was literally starving.

My tits were failing me.

My tits have always been my best quality. I'm not bragging when I say that. They are great, relative to the rest of my body, which is a gallery of horrors in comparison. There are so many problems with what's below my belly button there's not time enough to list them all (although unruly Medusa-like pubic hair is just the tip of the iceberg). By default my tits were my best girls, and historically the first things to be revealed on a first date or during a drunken game of strip dominoes.

The pediatrician suggested we switch to formula right away. Whoa, Dr. Cowboy. This is not my beautiful motherhood experience. I know what happens to children who don't breastfeed. They become drug addicts, serial killers, and socialites. I know that Michael Jordan was breast-fed until he was three and that Michael Jackson was not breast-fed at all. But since

I'm two hundred years too late to locate a wet nurse, I conceded to using formula until she had gained the requisite amount of weight, but it would end there. After that I was determined to breast-feed my child for one year. Minimum.

It was suggested I visit a lactation consultant by the name of Binky. If Binky wasn't available I was to see Corky. Those names are so real that I don't even have a joke to go with them.

We drove to Binky's office in Woodland Hills, and she proceeded to examine my breast-feeding technique.

Her findings? What was coming out of my nipples was something closer to puffs of milk-scented air than actual milk. My supply "sucked." That was the bad news. The good news is that it was the baby's fault, not mine.

The baby had a bad latch, which led to my breasts being engorged, which led to my milk supply drying up, which led to me sitting in a small office in Woodland Hills while a grown woman named Binky milked me. Yeah, that's right. She milked me.

Binky grabbed my nipple and pinched it hard—I know this sounds like porn for Teletubbies, but it was about as sexy as b'acne, which is to say not very—and jammed it about twelve inches into the baby's mouth. At that moment, the moment of my first proper latch, it became perfectly clear to me that my baby was part piranha. I'm not sure how I managed to conceive a child with a carnivorous freshwater fish from South America, but it seemed the only way to explain the excruciating pain.

I stamped my foot on the floor repeatedly. That was to keep me from punching my baby in the face. Truth is, I would not punch a baby, though I might wait until she's thirteen years old and give her one retroactively.

Two hours and several hundred dollars later, Binky sent us home with a hospital-grade pump, which I was to use every three hours until my supply could match my daughter's demand.

When we got home, the husband bottle-fed the baby while I zipped on my hands-free pumping bra, turned on the pump, and watched as it stretched my nipples through a transparent sleeve like Augustus Gloop going through the pipes of the chocolate river in *Willy Wonka*.

Now that I could actually see the milking process, I understood the problem. Milk wasn't flowing, it was eking out of my nipples, like beads of flop sweat. One hour of Hoover-strength milking left me with a grand total of a half ounce of milk. And most of that came from the right breast. The left was completely useless. If my right breast was a slacker, my left was its illiterate cousin who lost half his brain in a tragic pig-farming accident.

But I would not be beaten.

Over the next few weeks my husband bottle-fed our daughter, while I pumped every three to four hours for up to an hour at a time.

I learned all about galactagogues, which though it sounds like an alien form of governance is actually any substance that encourages lactation. As a result I ate oatmeal in large amounts, drank Guinness beer in small amounts, and ingested an herb that made my skin smell like a combination of maple syrup and curry. Mostly curry.

I took a prescription medication for reflux, one side effect of which is increased lactation, another side effect of which is depression. A hilarious situation for a new mother, if you think about it.

I went to breast-feeding support groups and listened to other new moms complain about their problems with overabundant flow, saying, "Ohmigod, I'm absolutely gushing. I could feed an army with what comes out of these." I smiled with empathy while imagining punching them in their overflowing tits.

And I pumped.

Until little by little, drop by drop, my milk started to flow—or at least dribble. Not nearly at the rate the child was drinking, but enough that I could supplement her formula feedings with a little of my own milky love.

I was winning. Soon we would be the very picture of skin-to-skin maternal bliss.

But as one slow-flowing nipple said to the other, "Not so fast."

The child did not want the breast.

When I offered my ever-so-feebly lactating nipple to my daughter, she would give it a look and a suck, and then scream into it like Henry Rollins yelling into a microphone. Worse, she could only be calmed by a pacifier. By a silicone version of my nipple.

This is what is known in the breast-feeding world as "nipple confusion," but if you asked my daughter, she would say there was no confusion. That savvy four-week-old knew exactly what she wanted, and she couldn't have been clearer if she'd e-mailed her thoughts to me and bcc'd her lawyer.

It was hard not to take it personally. Almost as hard as it is to saw through a silicone pacifier with a steak knife.

So I continued to pump around the clock and poured my liquid gold into little bottles that I or my husband would then feed her. I did this for four months, and that's when I gave up. As much as I believed in the benefits of breast-feeding, I believed that the six hours a day I was spending with the pump would be better spent with my child. So I 86'd the pump and decided to let nature take its course.

For a while I tried to fool her into sucking on my nipples. I'd make her laugh, and while her mouth was open I'd try jamming my nipple in there. But she never took to it; she'd just stare at me.

So now, two months later, my child is 100 percent formula-fed. She's healthy and growing, and I'm at peace with my choice. And that last part is a complete lie.

I am still tortured by it.

I still get a pang when I see a woman breast-feeding her baby, and invariably I stare for a few seconds too long and the woman gets up and moves away because she thinks I'm a pervert.

I worry.

I worry that there will be a chemical explosion and the city will be under siege by robots who take over the water supply and my baby will die because I won't be able to breast-feed her during the ensuing apocalypse.

I worry that she'll grow up to be a high school dropout and date a guy with a tattoo of a snake on his face who tries to rob a liquor store and in the process shoots and kills kindly old Sheriff Jenkins, and my dum-dum of a daughter will get blamed for it and end up on death row, where Susan Sarandon tries but ultimately fails to spare her life.

I worry that she'll become an asshole.

And that's why I still fight the daily urge to jam my dusty nipple in her mouth. I just hope I can get over it by the time she turns thirteen.

THE OTHER ONE

Eric Weinberg

MY SON BENJAMIN IS THREE and a half. He's an unbelievably sweet, smart, Spider-Man-obsessed kid who wakes up smiling and goes to bed asking me to lie next to him in the dark and tell him the story I made up about a monster who uses lemons and oranges and cherries and grapes and blueberries to make giant rainbows in the sky. (And sure, it occurs to me now that I've been sending my son to bed every night dreaming of an artistically inclined gay super-icon, but there's really no way to put that genie back in the bottle.) We're not religious people, but I think I can speak for my wife, Hilary, and say we feel really blessed to have Ben. So, that said, I want to talk about my second favorite son, Julian.

Just so you understand, I say "second favorite" only because

I don't love Julian as much as I love Ben. And I say "son" because he's not a daughter, which is what I really, really wanted. Badly. And I say "my" because I stubbornly choose to believe I helped produce him, despite the fact that he's almost a year and a half old and resembles me about as much as a slice of cheesecake resembles Jeff Goldblum.

When I say I don't love Julian as much as Benjamin, I'm really saying I don't know him as well: He's younger, his personality isn't as well formed, we haven't spent nearly as much time together. Plus, his head looks like a lightbulb. To be fair, it's not like the day Ben was born I loved him as much as I do now; I mean, I'm not crazy, or his mom. Point being, if I'm throwing a party, Ben gets an invite before Julian.

Back to how Julian's the wrong sex and probably not mine: See, whenever I thought about having children, I imagined a boy and a girl; it just seemed normal to me. For instance, *I'm* a boy and my *sister's* a girl. And, sure enough, Hilary's second pregnancy felt different than her first one. In fact, our doctor—who we asked not to tell us the sex of the baby right away—privately told Hilary's mother we were having a girl. Hilary's mom, who was also sworn to secrecy, told Hilary it was a girl. Then Hil and I had this great idea—well, copied this great idea—of having our doctor reveal the sex of our baby to us on a card, which we'd open over a romantic dinner. (Our romantic dinner was eaten at home, half-standing at the kitchen island while we went through junk mail, but I'm not saying that's mandatory.) Anyway, we opened the card to make it official, and it said, "Congratulations—it's a boy!" And, just like that, all the air left my body. Not in a farty way; I mean I was devastated. We *had* a boy, we had a *great* boy, what did we need another boy for? In hindsight, the card *should've* said, "Congratulations—it's a boy who should have you racing for a paternity test, except instead of being a man and having your worst fears confirmed, you'd rather spend the rest of your days doubting, always doubting." But I guess that would've been in poor taste.

Now, I'm no psychiatrist, but I am Jewish. So I've obsessed over this long enough to know that my desire for a baby girl probably goes back to me feeling a tad fucked-over by my older sister while I was growing up. (For the record, we're friends now, which I hope is encouraging to eight-year-olds everywhere.) As a kid it made me wish I had a younger sister, who I'd be far nicer to, and as an adult it made me wish I could have a little girl of my own to cuddle, to counsel, to connect with in the way that other fathers—my best friends, in fact—do with their daughters, just as mothers do with their sons. See, people always talk about that special relationship between a father and daughter; what they hardly ever talk about is that special relationship between a father and someone *else's* daughter. And, sure, I get that it's no one's idea of a classic May-December romance, but there's a certain bond you have with someone you've known since she pronounced that word "Dethember." My friend Brian in New York is having his daughter Zoe bat mitzvahed next month. A few weeks ago, Zoe grabbed the phone and told me that if I didn't come she was going to hunt me down and kill me. I laughed, and she said, "You think that's funny? What's funny is that I'm not kidding." So I'm going. And if my eyes tear up a little while I'm there, I'll tell everyone it's out of happiness.

Of course, when Hil was actually giving birth to Julian, all I was thinking was, *Just be healthy. And maybe have a vagina. Not in* addition *to a penis, because . . . anyway, just be healthy.* And he was healthy. He looked nothing like me, but I blew right past that until I had to tell the doctor my blood type, and he said, "Well, either you're wrong, or he's not your child." I blew past that, too, and as the weeks and months went by, I kept waiting for something, anything, familiar to show up in my second son. Instead, he just kept looking like some odd combination of my wife and . . . someone too fucking ugly for her to have slept with: He was pale and hairless, and I wouldn't describe his face as angelic so much as like a balloon that's losing air. "Maybe you should get a blood test," Hilary would joke with me. And we'd laugh, awkwardly. Friends trotted out something like "He really has your, um . . . expressions," because it's a nice thing to say, like "I love your house" or "I didn't realize you were that old." Yet oddly, over time, I've grown accustomed to Julian's face. Sometime last year I said, "Hey, handsome," and then he and I both did a double take when we realized I wasn't being sarcastic.

So, the upshot is, I have two boys. The Weinberg boys. As in "Mom, can the Weinberg boys come over?" Or "No arrests have been made, but local police are questioning the Weinberg boys about their parents' disappearance." And the thing is, Julian is *such* a boy: He grabs fistfuls of hair out of your scalp; he gashes himself over his eye and doesn't blink. And whereas when you pull Ben's hair back he almost has a pretty girl's face, when you pull Julian's hair back he just kind of looks like . . . well, suppose Andy Richter had chemo. Hil says we can always adopt a Chinese girl, but then my mind starts racing with all sorts of questions: Will she feel out of place going to school at Temple Israel? Won't she ruin the curve with her impossibly high academic standards? Will I always criticize her driving, and when did I become such an old-fashioned racist?

The truth is, love comes in all sorts of ways. With Julian,

well...I don't want to brag, but he pursued me. Big-time. It's almost embarrassing, when I think about it. "Oh, look who crapped himself—and I guess I'm the *only* one around who can change you." Maybe he knew that he'd wear me down, that eventually he'd win me over. Maybe he knew that proximity would lead to intimacy, the way it does for coworkers who spend too much time together, or for the houseguests on *Big Brother*. Anyway, he was right, because he made me fall completely in love with him. And it's not just a crush, it's the real thing, I can feel it.

The other morning, while I was brushing my teeth, Julian was in the living room with Hil when I suddenly heard crying. It wasn't just run-of-the-mill crying, it was the kind of shriek-ing, piercing, panicky cry that, as a parent, you somehow know brings with it bloody faces or broken bones. I rushed out to the living room yelling, "What happened?" "I put him down," Hilary explained. "Oh." I looked over at Julian's big wet eyes and his big red ears. My ears, I had to admit. I went back to the bathroom, wondering why this kid is so needy. This eighteen-month-old pink puddle of flesh who cries over nothing, who can barely say "mama" or "dada" or "baba," who can't feed or clothe himself, who can't walk five feet without falling over, who isn't even a *girl*, for Christ's sake...And I think, "Of course he's needy. He needs me." And I come back out of the bath-room, and I look at him, at his utterly boyish, blondish face, both foreign and familiar, smiling at me, at his body bending to me, at his arms reaching for me, and I'm a little shocked to realize, as I go to pick him up, that I need him, too.

WE'RE HAVING A MAYBE!

Cindy Chupack

'TWAS THE DAY AFTER CHRISTMAS, and I was reading *Newsweek*'s cover story on diet and fertility when I stood up, ripped the roof off a gingerbread house, and ate it, like Godzilla.

This was not something the cover story recommended, by the way. It was a reaction to something the cover story recommended, namely, that you shouldn't eat a lot of red meat if you're trying to get pregnant.

I was trying to get pregnant. My husband and I had been trying for two and a half years. I also had a steak on the grill, a petite filet that was going to be my lunch before I decided to have the gingerbread house instead.

"Trying" is a good word for this process. At first "trying" just meant sex without birth control, but when you marry at forty, "trying" quickly becomes more trying, and eventually we had the requisite army of experts, most of whom insurance doesn't cover, but of course, you can't put a price on a baby.

You *can* put a price on not having a baby. That's running us close to $45,000 in credit card debt.

So by the time I was reading that *Newsweek* article, I'd done it all—drugs, shots, suppositories, IUI, IVF, that test with the blue dye, acupuncture, stinky teas, human growth hormone injections... Once we were driving to see a doctor in Beverly Hills, and my husband asked what kind of doctor he was, and I said, "I don't know, but someone said to see him, so we're seeing him!" It was that doctor, incidentally, who told me to visualize my husband's face on a cartoon sperm, with arms welcoming my egg to him. We decided the guy was a quack, so I only saw him twice a week for about four months.

The thing is, when you're racing your biological clock, people can tell you pretty much anything and you'll do it. I still worry I need to track down some saint named Amachi so I can bring her red bananas. Recently a friend said something about inversions. Standing on your head. He wasn't sure if you were supposed to do it before sex, during, or just in general, but this worked for two women he knew, so I guess I have to stand on my head now. I'll probably visualize my husband's face on a cartoon sperm while I'm at it. Not because I'm on board with that. It's just a hard image to shake.

I do have limits, though. Several friends have highly recommended a fertility doctor in the Valley, but I will go to China for a baby before I go to the Valley.

My husband and I had become accustomed to paying people to tell us we weren't pregnant, so it was almost revolutionary that for the holidays this year, we made the decision to return to the old-fashioned method of not getting pregnant on our own.

We went to Jackson Hole, and we didn't even take ovulation sticks, which might not seem crazy to you people, but when you're in the middle of this madness, not knowing when you're ovulating is like not knowing where your cell phone is.

That was the idea. We wanted to lose ourselves for a while. We wanted to just have sex. Every day, you know, just in case, but even so, it was fun again, and that's how everyone says it finally worked for them, or for somebody they know, or for somebody somebody they know knows.

In the weeks after that trip, I felt good. Well, bad good. I mean, my breasts were tender, I felt a little nauseous, I was dead tired—I had all the bad good signs of pregnancy, which I recognized, because I'd been pregnant before.

We actually got pregnant on our honeymoon, and for a moment we were some of the people I now call "those people," people who got pregnant right away, maybe even accidentally (which now seems as likely to me as accidentally finding Osama bin Laden, but back then I didn't know what I know now any better). We were "those people" until three months later, when we found out the baby's head was too large, and there was fluid where there shouldn't be, and there was a malformed heart, and the baby probably wouldn't make it to term.

The doctor said we should seriously consider termination unless we were deeply religious. That news was hard to take, but even harder because I felt guilty. The truth is, at that time, I didn't want to be pregnant.

We'd just gotten married. I still wasn't sure it was going to last. I also thought a little time as a couple would be nice since it took us forty years to find each other.

But my husband was eager to start a family, so the morning after he proposed we were walking on the beach, and I threw my birth control pills into the ocean in a dramatic display of love and good faith, and it made him so happy that I had to resist the urge to run screaming into the surf to recover them.

I always wanted to have a baby . . . in five years. I'd been saying I wanted to have a baby in five years for about twenty years. I just never felt ready.

Ready or not, though, we conceived on our wedding night, and on day seven of our honeymoon I felt nauseous and, thinking I had a stomach bug, I stayed in our room.

We were in South Africa on a safari. They had warned us to keep the sliding doors to our bungalow locked because of the monkeys, but we hadn't seen any monkeys, and anyhow, I thought they meant we needed to keep the doors locked when we were out, and I was in, curled up in bed.

All of a sudden I heard the door open, and I called out, thinking it was my husband. Then I heard this *thump thump thump thump thump*, and I knew something wasn't right, so I got up and looked into the living room, and there were *seven monkeys*, throwing food around, and they froze as if I had just walked in on a teenagers' party. One was on a table by a big bowl of fruit, and it just stared at me, holding an apple, midbite. The funny thing, looking back, was that this was my fear. This is what I thought it would be like to have children. This is why I never felt ready.

Cut to the day of the termination. We were already distraught, and then on the way to the appointment, we got pulled over by the police because my husband didn't see a woman walk into the crosswalk. I did see the woman, but she was on the other side of the street, plus I was trying not to say anything as my husband had taken to charging me five dollars every time I told him how to drive, but the policeman pulled us over and said, "Are you trying to kill someone?!"

I was thinking, *Yes, that's exactly what we're trying to do, and if you would let us go, we could get on with it.*

I remember that the rest of the way to the clinic I was pissed at my husband for not seeing the woman, and he was pissed at the policeman for being such a dick, and the truth was, we were both just pissed at the universe for giving us this gift that we had to return.

Now, thanks to Jackson Hole, we were getting a second chance. This time, when I took the pregnancy test, I was praying for a positive result rather than dreading it. But, of course, it was negative.

That was in the morning, and then a few hours later I was reading *Newsweek*, and the next thing I knew, I was eating a gingerbread house.

The gingerbread itself was pretty hard. I think it was made in Korea and not meant for eating, although that was never explicitly stated, just as it's not explicitly stated that you shouldn't eat candles. Some things you're just supposed to know. It came from a kit, one of six kits my friend purchased for a gingerbread house decorating party, so I had decorated alongside five women who were all mothers, some several times over, one with her newborn son in tow, and I know it's not a competition, but my gingerbread house was the best.

Sure, these ladies had kids, but I had the Sistine Chapel of gingerbread houses. And I was proud of it, as sad as that might be. So just factor that in when you're imagining me eating it, like Godzilla. It was like eating my young, since, as we've established, I had no actual young.

I had decorated the roof with white icing, little sour balls, red Twizzlers, and green gumdrops, none of which tasted very good. What I really wanted was the door, which was made of Hershey's Special Dark Chocolate.

Maybe you're wondering why I didn't just pull the door off. Well, I tried that, but the icing for these things is like glue, and the door was stuck to the front of the house, and the whole house was stuck to a foil-covered piece of cardboard, so you had to eat the roof before you could eat the door.

Well, you didn't have to *eat* the roof. You could, I suppose, just rip it off. But I was upset for all the reasons I've mentioned, and red meat was the final straw.

See, not only did I have a steak on the grill, I'd had a steak on the grill almost every day for the past year. Diet, for me, had been the most rewarding and punishing part of this baby quest. I'd gone from my highest weight ever to my lowest weight ever, because I didn't want to go from my highest weight ever to an even higher weight during pregnancy, since that would mean spending the rest of my life in caftans. I had a lot of fears about what becoming a parent would do to my career and my life (monkeys in the room!), so I wanted to at least limit what it could do to my wardrobe. Plus it was supposed to be healthier to get pregnant at a healthier weight.

So I went on a supervised diet with someone we will just call Dr. Skinny. His office is powder blue with white molding, and the whole thing looks like a Wedgwood plate. He is tall and thin (only 6 percent body fat! he will tell you), and he wears bad blue suits (from K-mart! he will tell you) and I suspect he wears a toupee, but I was never able to confirm this. He confirms your need to lose weight by pinching your sides with his fingers, so I should have just reached out and grabbed his hair one day in retaliation.

Dr. Skinny is basically an obesity doctor, so I was hoping when I went to the first group meeting that he and the group would say, "What are you doing here?" Instead, he snapped my "before" picture, and the next thing I knew, I was weighing my food at restaurants and doing lines of Splenda in the bathroom.

The Dr. Skinny diet is called an eating plan, but it's really a not-eating plan. It definitely works, but it's very strict. You're not allowed a gingerbread house, that's for sure. It's basically protein and vegetables with Wasa crackers thrown in for survival. You only get two meals a day, only three ounces of protein per meal, so I decided my protein would be filet mignon whenever possible.

My plan was to lose weight until I got pregnant, but since it was taking so fucking long to get pregnant, I ate a lot of red meat, and I lost a lot of weight. Fifty pounds, to be exact.

For the first time ever, I felt like someone who belonged in L.A. I bought a pair of skinny jeans and strutted my significantly smaller stuff down Robertson Boulevard. I felt, in a word, fabulous. So fabulous, in fact, it took me a while to notice that I wasn't getting my period—and not for the reason I'd been hoping.

As annoying and depressing as it is to get your period each month when you're trying to get pregnant, it's nothing compared to *not* getting your period for *five* months when you're trying to get pregnant. My ovaries—like the screenwriters guild—were on strike.

So although I loved my skinny jeans, I didn't love them

enough to give up having a baby, and I still don't think it's fair that that might be the price I have to pay for wearing them. I thought $178 was expensive! It's like I made a deal with the skinny devil.

I did thankfully get my period back once I went off my not-eating plan, which I did with the gusto of someone who's been told to gain weight for a role, and thanks to Dr. Dao, who suggested "electro-acupuncture" to jump-start my ovaries.

That was another mistake I'd made. I'd left Dr. Dao of "Mao and Dao" at the Tao of Wellness six months earlier. If you've ever tried to get pregnant in Los Angeles, someone probably recommended going to them for acupuncture, and it's worth it, if only for the friendly desk staff, soothing music, heat lamps, and weekly nap. I loved Dr. Dao, but I only saw him once a month. The other three visits each month I saw another doctor in the practice, who was very nice, but he didn't show after my first IVF attempt failed, and he didn't show again the next week, so not only was I forced to see someone who wasn't even Asian, I found out the reason he didn't show was that his wife had just had her second baby. Like I said, I know it's not a competition, but I was annoyed this nice man was sticking needles in me, and in all these other women, listening to our fertility problems, while at home, his wife was just pushing 'em out.

I'm not saying this was rational. I'm not saying it was pretty. But I left Dr. Dao's practice for a female acupuncturist, and I immediately regretted it. She forgot every week why I was there, so I had to explain each time about how I hadn't had a period for two, then three, then four, then five months, and each time she reacted with horror. "Five months?!" Also, her receptionist was downright surly.

So I finally returned, contrite, to Dr. Dao, and he agreed we needed to jump-start my ovaries, which, I'm not kidding, involved tiny little spark plugs that attached to the needles they put in my stomach and caused a zap-zap-zap sensation.

There was a control that changed the speed and intensity of the zap-zap-zap. Usually Dr. Dao would set the dial, but once he left me alone with it and let me control it, and that's when I wondered if maybe I was in some sort of cruel medical experiment where they try to figure out how far a woman will go to have a baby. Will she stand on her head? Lose fifty pounds? Blow up her ovaries? Keep turning it up until . . . *poof!*

Because really, how much disappointment can one woman take? How many times can you be hopeful when odds are you're going to get sucker punched by your period or a negative pregnancy test or something else you never saw coming?

And yet you can't stress about that, because stress is the worst thing for fertility.

I know, by the way, that once you have a baby, this all gets put behind you. I know the end of this movie. I don't know where or when or how. My fertility doctor broached the idea of donor eggs, but I don't really like guests in my house, so in my womb . . . I don't know.

But that's the point. You don't know. You don't know what dream you'll be willing to abandon and what dream you'll be willing to adopt. You only know that once you have your baby, the movie will be rewritten so that is the only possible ending, the only baby for you, and for now, you're just slogging your way through the second act.

Which you have to do, I guess. As in any worthwhile endeavor, you have to go through the hard, unsavory part before you get to the good stuff. You have to eat the roof before you can eat the door.

TEN MONTHS IN

Jason Nash

I FUCKING HATE HAVING A kid. I'm sorry, but I really do. I really hate it so much sometimes. I want my life back so badly.

Let me tell you, Tom Cruise owes Brooke Shields an apology, because postpartum is alive and well and I've got it. From not being able to go to the movies. From not being able to sleep past seven in the morning. From the fact that if I let my wife go to the gym, she doesn't count her time showering and drying her hair as hours where I'm watching the baby.

I want to run to Mexico. I mean literally, go to Niketown, buy $130 sneakers and really good socks, and run to fucking Mexico. And when I get to the border, the guard will say, "What's your business here?" And I'll say, "Abandoning my wife and baby." He'll grab my papers. "You can't do that!" Then I'll stab him in the gut with a knife and keep running until I find a job teaching scuba diving. (I know nothing about scuba diving.)

I want to jump a train cross-country and eat beans with hobos while listening to *The Eagles, Volume 2* on a boom box covered in splattered paint.

I want to sing. Not to be a pop singer. I want to move to Vermont and grow a beard and earn my room and board at a bed-and-breakfast playing a Billy Joel songbook nightly. (I also know nothing about piano and have failed at learning many times, and people don't really like my singing. I know this because it's usually met with someone saying, "Um, can you stop doing that?" Maybe it's the songs I'm choosing, but as far as I'm concerned nothing brightens the soul like a few bars of Christina Aguilera's "I Am Beautiful.")

So why did I have a baby? Well, the woman I married was four years older than me with a ticking biological clock. It was put to me like this: "Now's my only chance." What a fucked-up trump card pity party of an excuse that is you women use.

"Honey, I really don't want a baby at this point in my life," I pleaded with my wife.

"God's stealing my eggs," my wife said.

How else can you respond to that except to say, "Let's go look at cribs"? You certainly can't say, for instance, "Why didn't you have your kids in your twenties when you knew you had plenty of time?" or "Did your closest girlfriend let you in on this secret at your thirty-seventh birthday party?"

More reasons why I didn't want the kid: I had a horrible childhood, and my father terrorized me as a boy. The kind of dad who would pummel you when you ripped your pants or spilled milk at the table. The kind of dad who would stand right behind home plate and criticize your every move while you batted so that it was impossible for you to make contact with the ball. Zero for four on days he was there. Two for four on days he wasn't.

"How come you don't do well when I'm there?" he'd ask.

"I don't know, Lou Holtz, maybe it's because you put the fear of God in me?"

Most important, I'm angry, just like my dad was. Angry that I'm not further along in my career. Angry that I've worked hard and can't make a dent in this town. Angry that after all my efforts I turned into him, a guy with a lot of potential who can't seem to get things off the ground. Why would I or anyone want to put that on a kid?

Still, I did it anyway, impregnating my wife on our first try. For once, I was actually good at something.

I dreaded the months before birth, counting my last days of freedom like Ed Norton in *The 25th Hour*.

"What do you think of this stroller?" my wife asked one day while shopping.

"Oh, it's great because there's a compartment underneath for all my hopes and dreams. There's even a lockbox so they're close by, but you can't really get to them. Sort of like phantom pain."

Also, I hated fucking my wife while she was pregnant. It wasn't because she didn't look beautiful to me, but I couldn't get past the image of hitting the kid in the face with my penis over and over again. As if Cheech Marin's voice would spring out from inside her vagina in the middle of the act: "Hey, man! Someone's in here!"

I love my child, and he's the cutest kid in the world, but I didn't want one. Ten months in I still don't want one, but I did it fully believing that what's difficult in life must be good for you.

When you're pregnant, most fathers try to talk you out of your fears of hating your baby by telling you that once you hold the baby, a paternal hormone kicks in.

"Don't worry," my friend Don said. "When you get that baby in your arms it's just like God and nature, man. Something kicks in and it all feels so right."

Well, a few days out of the hospital, I was sitting in that rocking chair and feeding him and looking into his eyes—I mean, really connecting with him, the moment finally there—and I thought, *This fucking blows. I hate this shit. I knew I would hate this! What the fuck was Don talking about? Don is a fucking asshole. You know what? I've never liked Don.*

That's why having a baby is a lot like that book *The Da Vinci Code.* A few summers ago, everybody was running around telling me, "You have to read *The Da Vinci Code!*" And I kept saying, "Really? Because I don't think I'm going to like *The Da Vinci Code.*" And you read it and it blows. You say, *This is a book for everybody, and you know what, I'm not everybody.* I don't like Starbucks, I don't dig Grisham novels, and procreating is not my cup of tea.

My wife and I fight nonstop since he was born. To her credit she is smart, calculated, and a formidable opponent. People always say you should marry your equal, a person who challenges you. This is bullshit. I married my equal and it's a fucking bloodbath every day. Do you know who's also pretty equal? The Israelis and the Palestinians. Nobody's quitting that war anytime soon.

You're also tired all the time when you have a baby, so you do dumb things. There's tons of hand sanitizer around to keep the baby clean. One night, I accidentally masturbated in the dark with Purell instead of Astroglide, because they come in remarkably similar bottles. Eddie Murphy has a bit about this, and let me just say, no matter how tall or how long you are, it's actually very difficult to wash your dick in the bathroom sink.

Most of all, I miss my wife. We used to have the best time together. Now, when I see her, she just tells me things I'm doing wrong. Granted, I have no credibility as a father.

In my defense, she also thinks the worst is going to happen at any moment.

"Do you hear the shower upstairs?" she'll ask.

"No."

"Do you think he got out of his crib?"

"And took a shower? I don't know, did you not give him a bath before bed? Maybe he pulled a muscle and wanted to get a kink out of his neck?"

These are all silly complaints about the baby. But one day, my worst fear came true. My anger surfaced. I had just found out that I didn't get a job as a writer on a very shitty TV show, and I really needed the money. I worked hard on the submission and was told my material was not up to snuff. *Really? Have you watched the show you put on every night?* I thought, after hanging up with my agent.

My son started crying and wouldn't stop. My failure, my life, the feeling that everything was finished came to a head.

I put my son down in his crib. Then, enraged, I punched a giant hole through the door to his room. One time. *Boom!* Again. *Boom!* And again. Screaming "Fuck!" each time, letting everything out. I knew I was doing it. I knew I wasn't hurting the baby, but I was so mad I wanted my wife to see my anger. I wanted to tell her, "You took my fucking life away and this is what you get. A hole in the door of your perfect baby's room, in your perfect house."

And I turned and saw my son and he was so scared. And for the first time, it clicked. That I was wrong. That I was a part of something larger now. That I was being a selfish fuck and it didn't matter how my career ended up. I grabbed him, held him, and just cried. The next week I went into therapy and started a massive overhaul of myself.

I gotta make it work. I gotta be good. Gotta remember that this is what life is all about.

The best part is, now when I give him a bath, I sing at the top of my lungs. And he sings back, ten months old and just as out of key.

SMILE!

Julie Rottenberg

I'VE ALWAYS HAD TROUBLE MAKING decisions. I can stare at a menu for a good half hour and still, when the waiter comes over, I can't decide between the fish and the pasta.

I had the same trouble deciding whether to have kids. Of course, you can't send back the kids with the ease or frequency that I tend to send my food back to the kitchen, so I basically spent a decade between the ages of twenty-five and thirty-five paralyzed by ambivalence about whether or not to become a parent.

Now you'd think, given that so many people have kids, somebody might have been able to shed some light on my dilemma. Nope. Every parent I knew fed me the same hyper yet robotic chant of "Oh, you have to! Best thing I ever did. Changed my life forever."

But I'm no dummy. I could see through their glassy, sleep-deprived eyes and notice that they'd become malnourished and that their marriages had gone from sexy and fun to angry and naggy. In fact, the more I heard that "Oh, you have to!" mantra, the more I started to think that having kids must be so godawful bad, these poor people had no choice but to repeat to themselves again and again that what they did wasn't a huge mistake, that it was for the best, that it "changed their lives forever."

Every time I imagined having kids, I burst into tears, or into a cold, panicky sweat. All I could connect to was the loss of it all: loss of independence, youth, sleep; loss of life as I knew and loved it. But my husband, Ben, knew he wanted a family, and eventually I decided that while I might never be ready to have a baby, my fear of waking up one day and regretting that choice was even scarier.

Looking back on all that anguish and indecision, it's actually hilarious to me now. Ahh, to have the luxury of ambivalence! Turns out the quickest remedy for ambivalence is discovering you may not even be able to do this thing you're so fucking ambivalent about. Yes, I am happy to report that my ambivalence was cured, and all it took was six miscarriages in a row. My panic about how life might change for the worse if I had kids was replaced by a whiplash-like panic that I might never be lucky enough to find out.

So by the time we were finally able to bring our baby girl home from the hospital, I felt I was in the unique position of having both a keen understanding of the downside of parenting and the religious gratefulness that only a hellish odyssey through the world of infertility can produce. I was armed and ready for anything this baby could give me.

I won't even bother trying to describe how much Thelma cried in those first few weeks, because I now understand that like pain, unless you're experiencing it in that very moment, it's really impossible to convey. "Thelma cried all night last night" is really just words: nouns, a verb, an adjective or two. It can't communicate the teeth-rattling, heart-racing, brain-twisting mania I experienced as she cried for hours on end, night after night, for reasons we could not ascertain. A life-long control freak, I felt totally out of control.

Naturally, everyone had advice for us. "Are you singing to her?" Of course I was singing to her. Since I didn't know the words to any lullabies, I went to my go-to area, show tunes. The soothing, calm ones, of course: "There's a place for us, somewhere a place for us..." I grew up listening to *West Side Story*, and I've probably heard that song a thousand times, but only now, in the 3:00 A.M. postpartum darkness of my Brooklyn living room, did I start thinking about how profoundly sad it is. Poor Tony and Maria are so deluded in their hope and optimism. There *wasn't* a place for them, there *wasn't* a time for them. Tony died in Maria's arms thanks to senseless gang rivalry and Anita's big mouth. Then that got me thinking about Tony and Maria's ancestors Romeo and Juliet, who also died because of a total misunderstanding—a communication glitch that would be sitcom-worthy if it weren't so tragic. I was suddenly overwhelmed by how scary and heartbreaking life is. So there I was, singing this incredibly sad song to my baby, expecting her not to cry. But now I was crying, too, hard. For Maria. For Tony. For Thelma. For me.

I realized, as I applied big, cold cabbage leaves to my breasts to soothe my chafed nipples, that everything I had feared all those years about having a baby was true—but of all those fears, which were mostly about what I would lose, the one I never talked about or even admitted to myself was the fear of what I might gain: that if I ever did have a baby, I might care so much, maybe too much, and that's what I was really afraid of.

So! I tried switching to some more upbeat tunes: "You are my sunshine, my only sunshine..." Even this, when sung against the backdrop of a screaming baby in the middle of the night, took on dark and ominous tones. That high note of "you make me hap-*peee*" always killed me, and I would inevitably break down in tears just as I hit it. (It's very hard to sing when you're crying.) Again, it was as if I were stoned and hearing the lyrics for the first time. "La-la-la-la, dear, how much I love you..." *Well, oh my God,* I realized, *that is just so true! I didn't understand how much my mother loved me until now, and Thelma won't know how much I love her until she has a baby—which maybe she won't ever have, which would be okay, I would understand— because I almost didn't!* Then I would lose it again. There we were, night after night, Thelma and I, crying together. It was like a cry-along. Let's see who can cry the loudest!

In my whole pre-baby life, I was always incredibly judgmental about parents who couldn't stand to hear their babies cry. I was a big believer in letting them "cry it out" and was eager to put that to use. When we consulted the doctor, though, she informed us that it was waaaay too early for that, that a baby that young can't learn anything yet. I thought, *Great. She's too young, we're too old; everybody's crying, nobody's learning.* In case we weren't convinced by the doctor's warning, we then heard on 20/20 that if a baby is left to cry too long, it secretes some crazy

hormone in the brain that can lead to—and I quote—"Hitler."
Yes, there's a Hitler hormone. We were turning our baby into
Hitler. This theory was supported by the unsettling observa-
tion that when Thelma did fall asleep in her basket, one of her
arms would inevitably escape the swaddle to assume what can
only be described as the Heil Hitler salute. We decided this was
our punishment for giving her the world's longest, Jewiest last
name: Rubin-Rottenberg.

The advice kept pouring in: "Motion, motion, they love the
motion!" So I would charge down the street, pushing her in
her stroller, passing all these other Park Slope parents with
their smiling babies happily enveloped in their goddamned
slings. Why weren't these babies crying? I couldn't understand
it. As I whizzed by, I would shout out, "How old?" "How old?"
But I never stopped moving long enough to hear the answer.

I didn't care about Thelma hitting any developmental marks
except for one: At around six weeks, I became obsessed with
her smiling—or rather, the fact that she wasn't smiling. A
friend asked, "Well, are you smiling at her?" *Umm, yes, when
I'm not crying.* I started spending an uncomfortable amount
of time smiling at Thelma. I was like a crazed happy-sad clown,
putting on these creepy forced smiles and saying through
gritted teeth, "Smile! Smile! Smile!" I tried everything: slap-
stick, kooky faces, crazy voices—but I got nothing.

At the next doctor's visit, they were all very impressed by
Thelma's motor skills. "Look! She can already hold her head
up! Look how strong she is!" I didn't care about any of that.
What did it matter that she could hold her head up if she wasn't
smiling when it was up? Who cares about physical strength if
she can't appreciate a well-crafted joke? I became convinced
that Thelma might never smile, might never stop crying, might

never sleep. That she would be the first baby who just cried through life and was always awake.

Naturally, I was wrong. Thelma did smile. I thought I might have imagined it, but then she smiled again. And the smiles got bigger and bigger, and then she started laughing, and she hasn't stopped since. And in the same way that you can't describe the pain of hearing your baby scream, I won't attempt to describe how it feels when I see that big, openmouthed smile. People said, "You won't remember those first few grueling months," but they're wrong. I will never forget them. Because of them, every smile, every peaceful night that Thelma sleeps through, every moment she's awake and *not* crying, means so much more.

As for all those people who said, "Best thing I ever did" and "Changed my life forever"—well, I'm willing to acknowledge that maybe they weren't all overcompensating for some dark, cynical truth underneath their giddiness. Still, for whatever reason, I needed to wrestle with the question of whether to have a baby for as long as I did. Maybe that's what I was mourning all those nights of crying with Thelma. That single question that loomed so large in my life, that practically defined me, doesn't exist anymore. Naturally, I've moved on to other questions. After all, I haven't left my old self completely behind. I'm still skeptical and judgmental and careful not to sound too gooey when I talk about Thelma. But I'm also honest enough to admit: I'm awfully glad she's here.

BOYS DON'T CRY

Mike Sikowitz

"HILARY SWANK CAN*not* CARRY A romantic comedy." That's not my opinion. I happen to have found her quite winning in two of the best romantic comedies of the last decade, *Million Dollar Baby* and *The Reaping*. No, as unlikely as it may seem, the preceding opinion was actually shared with me by one of Los Angeles's most respected mohels—or, for the few of you not in entertainment, "Jewish men who perform circumcisions." Even more oddly, this criticism of Hilary Swank was levied by the mohel at the exact moment he was giving my newborn son what my older son refers to as a Jewish penis.

I am, by trade, a comedy writer. And I'm writing about circumcision here. But despite the expectations generated when you let a comedy writer loose on a bris, you'll not be hearing jokes about "Give us the emerald cut," "Can we get ten percent off?," "Do you have a girl's name picked out, just in case?," "I'm sorry, did I cut you off?," or "Remember, I work for tips!" I hoped not to hear any of this type of joke at our second son's bris, either. Because if there's one thing I can tell you about my wife, Bonnie, and me, when we pay someone to mutilate our baby's genitals, we don't want shtick.

Before I continue, I want to make one thing clear: I'm not out to malign our mohel. In fact, we recommend him highly, if you're in the market for someone to slice your baby's junk. But, as I will be making a gentle complaint about one aspect of his approach, I think it's only fair to protect his identity by fictionalizing his name. So for our purposes, I'm talking about the well-known mohel Kevin Murphy.

Now, for our older son's bris, we also went Murphy. Bonnie is a thorough researcher, and she'd found that there are certain mohels in Los Angeles, like Moskowitz, Beninfeld, and Murphy, who are also doctors and, as such, are licensed to administer anesthesia. This appealed, because, if there's a second thing I can tell you about us, it's that when we pay someone to mutilate our baby's genitals, we'd prefer that it not hurt more than necessary. In fact, thinking back to our first date, I think those two things were what brought Bonnie and me together initially.

Our sons were born five years apart. You know, Jewish twins. (Get it? Because, unlike the Irish, we as a people aren't all that sexually vigorous?) Also, our first son came five weeks early, so much of that experience, and the events surrounding it, is a blur for me. However, I do remember that the bris Murphy performed was top drawer, to borrow a phrase from the Princeton graduating class of 1926. He was warm and professional and brought to the event a tone that fit perfectly with our style of Judaism, which can best be described as reformed, or, more specifically, culturally-involved-but-spiritually-lapsed-agnostic-but-not-so-sure-of-our-doubts-that-we-don't-fear-that-we-might-be-wrong...ism. In other words, while we have issues with the religion, and some healthy skepticism about the bigger questions, it's important to us that our sons, and their penises, be brought up Jewish.

Our second son's bris was a different story. A story that took place this year, 2008, on the morning of the twenty-seventh day of the Jewish month of Tevet—although it was unseasonably warm, so it felt more like Adar, or even Tishri. You know, global warming. See, what either didn't present itself five years earlier or somehow escaped my memory was Murphy's fascination with "the Biz."

For those of you who are bris-uninitiated, what generally happens is, the mohel says some prayers in Hebrew, performs the ritual circumcision, and then everyone eats bagels and the men eventually stop cringing. What's different about a Murphy bris is that he basically does the work beforehand. He gives the baby anesthesia, then performs the bulk of the procedure in private, with only one or both of the parents present—in this case just me. Somehow, I wasn't squeamish about the scalpel, or the blood flowing from my son's tiny bay shrimp of a wiener. Maybe because I positioned myself with my back to the action and proceeded to lock my neck in place to make sure I wouldn't see anything, even accidentally. It was at this moment—when a Jewish father has entrusted the mohel with fulfilling his sacred covenant with God—when Murphy turned to me and asked a question filled with reverence and introspection. "So. How's the strike treating you?"

Granted, it was a fair question. The strike he was referring to, of course, was the Writers Strike of 2007–'08, in which Hollywood's TV and film writers decided, en masse, to stop working in the hopes of gaining a share of future profits that would be generated when the companies who produce their work figured out how to make any using the Internet and other emerging technologies. All of this had been on my mind on the days leading up to, and the days following, my son's bris. I'd expected that this special day would provide a respite from stressful strike talk. With any other mohel, maybe. But not Murphy. So there we were, just him, me, and my son in the room. There was awkward silence. He might just as well have been saying, "How 'bout this weather?"—if we were in a city that actually had any.

So I told him, as briefly as I knew how, that the strike was a bummer and that, not unlike what my son was going through, I was hopeful it would be over soon, with no lasting damage.

What I didn't realize was that the man operating on my son's penis was actually Army Archerd.

"So, do you think it's the right thing?" he continued.

"Oh, yeah. I mean, we're not that religious, but we think it's important that his penis look like his brother's, and his daddy's."

"No, I mean the strike."

"Oh. Um, well, I'm not that involved in all the issues, but I hope it's the right thing."

"Me, too. I'll be honest with you, it's not great for business." I was surprised to hear that brises were actually a place where people were . . . cutting back.

"So, what were you working on before the strike?" he asked.

It was becoming clear to me that this was not going to stop

anytime soon. Now, there's something in my DNA, some kind of supergene for politeness, which prevents me from saying, "I'd rather not discuss this now." However, it doesn't prevent me from trying to indicate that with body language, tone of voice, and every available fiber of my being.

"Oh, I just finished a show for Fox called *Unhitched*."

"What was it about?"

"Four friends in their thirties who are newly out of long-term relationships."

"Sounds interesting."

"Well, it's okay."

"What was the order for?"

"Six episodes."

"Man, those orders just keep getting smaller. I remember when people used to get thirteen, on air, with huge penalties. Those days are gone, huh?"

"It would seem that way."

"You know, I've had a sitcom idea for the longest time. How do you go about pitching a sitcom?"

"Uh, I just try to briefly give a sense of the characters, the world they live in, and the different places the show could go."

"That makes sense. I could tell you the idea, if you want. It's edgy."

"You know, I'm not sure this is the best—"

"There's these two families. On the Lower East Side of Manhattan. One owns a deli, the other a dry-cleaning business next door to the deli. Now for years, it's been like the Hatfields and the McCoys: 'Your dry-cleaning chemicals leak into our kitchen!' 'All the clothes we clean smell like pickles!' You get the idea."

"Sure. Lotta potential there."

"But here's the hook: The college-aged daughter of the deli family falls in love with the college-aged son of the dry-cleaning family."

"Ah. So kind of a Romeo and Juliet."

"Yes. But fresher!"

I stand there, smiling congenially, thinking, *This is the hackiest, dustiest idea I've ever heard. Still, with the right casting . . .*

"Well, you're the writer, not me," he conceded.

"Yup," I agreed, although at the moment, I was less a writer and more a guy who'd actually taken to looking at genital mutilation as a way to take my mind off the conversation.

"And your wife. She's a writer, too, I recall?"

"Yup." Apparently, the conversation had a sequel.

"What's she working on?"

"Well, a movie she wrote is coming out this summer."

"Ahh, good for her. What genre?"

"Romantic comedy."

"Who's in it?"

"It stars Uma Thurman."

"I love Uma Thurman. So great with the physical stuff."

"That she is."

"You know, my wife and I just saw this *P.S. I Love You*. Have you seen it yet?"

"No."

"Well, walk, don't run, know what I'm saying?"

"Yes, you're saying you didn't care for it."

"I'll tell you something. Hilary Swank can*not* carry a romantic comedy."

Eventually, as impossible as it seemed, the special bris edition of *Access Hollywood* ended. From there, we went downstairs, where a group of close friends and family had gathered, and Murphy performed the remainder of the ceremony. Just as he had been five years before, he was sweet, warm, and welcoming—and I remembered why we used him again.

After it was all over and the last of the guests had departed, I held our beautiful baby in my arms and tried to make sense of the whole thing. Even though he was fast asleep, I felt a need to try to impart some fatherly wisdom to him on this momentous day.

So I told him, "Look: It's not a perfect world you were just born into. Sometimes you get the best mohel money can hire, and he chews your ear about show biz for a half hour. Sometimes your son falls in love with the daughter of your nemesis, the deli owner, and all you can do is sit back and watch the hilarity ensue. Sometimes you can win an Academy Award for an earnest boxing tear-jerker, and yet you can't even hold your own opposite Gerard Butler in an insipid piece of fluff. But the important thing to remember is that, from this day forward, you and I will always have matching junk."

SWEET DREAMS

Caroline Bicks

L.A. MAY BE THE CITY of dreams, but for us parents, Boston is the city of sleep. All of the greatest pediatric sleep doctors practice there. You can feel the pulse of their giant brain-veins as you drive down Longwood Ave. and Storrow Drive, past the medical Walk of Fame: Boston Children's, Beth Israel, Mass General, Dana-Farber. Homes to the greatest baby doctors on earth. So great, you know them by one name, like Bono, or Angelina, or God. To us, they are superstars: Sears, Brazelton, and, of course, the great Ferber. The man who made "cry it out" a household phrase. A man so famous that he has his own verb: Ferberize. As in "We can't go out tonight, we're Ferberizing little Max."

Ferberizing is the Ironman of competitive parenting: You

train your baby to sleep on his own by letting him scream his little lungs out all alone wondering where the hell you went. It's not for the weak or the lazy.

But if you have the stony heart to do it, it's worth it. Because, as every overachieving parent knows, it's all about the sleep: how soon your child does it through the night, how long, and how deeply. It's the single biggest mark of success or failure in the first three months of parenthood. The faster you reach it, the sooner little Max can get on with tracking a raisin with his eyes and packing his bags for Harvard.

So, naturally, if you live in Boston and you want your child to have an edge, you try to get a piece of the sleep doctors. Anxious and overeducated, we'll line up, like Oscar Day gawkers, to catch a glimpse of the great ones—to hear them speak, or to rub elbows with them at your husband's boss's college roommate who went to med school with one of them's cocktail party.

Some parents might even have the balls to seek an appointment. Fat chance. Someone has to actually die before a space opens up, and even then there are parents who've been waiting years ahead of you. Get in line, groupie. You can't sleep your way to the sleep doctors in this town.

You need to know all this so you can appreciate what it is I'm about to tell you. I'm not a lucky person. I don't win preschool raffles or baby-shower games or Blue's Clues Bingo. But one day—one frigid New England Monday—my luck changed. I got the golden ticket of competitive parenting.

My daughter hadn't slept through the night in four and a half years. In other words, never. For a while we were able to make excuses for her: "Oh, she needs to eat every few hours"; or "We just moved, so she's in a transition period"; or "It's Daylight Savings. Again." Every few months we'd buy another sleep book, read it, and try the latest method out on her for a week or so, but none of them ever took. Then we'd get too tired, or lose the book, and things would just keep on keeping on.

We never volunteered any of this information, but inevitably we would get asked the Question: "Is she sleeping through the night?" Now, this is a land mine of a question. It seems harmless, but what the person really wants to know is, "Are you a lazy slacker?" or, if they're newish parents, "Are you worse at this than I am?" The few times we fell into the trap of telling people the truth, they'd start in about setting limits and consistency. Usually this would be followed by a lecture on their personal sleep guru's philosophy and how, with the right commitment, it worked for them.

The point is, no one feels sorry for you when your kid is the "Bad Sleeper." They just look at you like you represent everything that's wrong with the world: negligence, sloth, incompetence. Like I can't be bothered with sleep training because I'm too busy surfing the Internet for cheap deals on recalled car seats. To make things worse, every time we turned around there'd be another study out about how sleep deprivation makes you stupid and fat. Great. Now we weren't just lame. We were dumb, fat, *and* lame.

One day, determined to seize control, we locked our daughter in her room and let her scream from three thirty to six o'clock in the morning. Just like the book said. When she finally stopped, our stony hearts leapt for joy. We cracked open the door, expecting to find her little body in a heap on the floor, surrendered to sleep. Instead, there she stood, staring at us with a twinkle in her eye—baby shit everywhere. If I hadn't been so completely freaked out, I might have admired her for her ingenuity. After all, she figured out what the biggest weapon in her toddler arsenal was, and she wasn't afraid to use it. But as I pulled on my rubber gloves and started scrubbing the walls with every ounce of disinfectant I could find in the house, all I could hear was the snide voice of Failure whispering in my ear: *It's over. She's broken you. You just don't have what it takes.*

We started lying to friends and relatives after that. We figured if we couldn't wipe out Failure, we could hide it like a fifth of scotch in the flour bin.

But then our son was born, and I stopped being able to keep up whatever facade of control I'd managed to cobble together. The interrupted sleep combined with a newborn was finally just too much. I started doing things like leaving the house with my Brest Friend still on. A Brest Friend, if you haven't seen one, is a big foam doughnut that Velcros around your waist so you can rest the baby on it, breast-feed, and keep your hands free for things like eating and crying. It even has little pockets in it for the remote and your cell phone in case you want to watch people on TV eating and crying; or want to talk to a friend and cry, or talk to her about what you're eating.

I don't know if it was the hormones or the sense of our utter failure finally hitting me that drove me to chance the unthinkable. Anyway, one day, Brest Friend strapped to my waist, boobs flapping around like a crazed harpy's, I fished out my phone and called the office of the Great Dr. Ferber himself.

There must have been something in my voice—some soundwave frequency that vibrated in just the right way off the receptionist's inner ear. Kind of like a dying whale sending out a distress call. Maybe someone had just that second died and, before the receptionist had had time to pick up the phone to call the next family in line, my call had gone through. All I know is that she had an appointment for me. Six months away in July, but still, an appointment. And not with one of his lackeys, or his protégés. With Him.

I carried that appointment around with me like a sweet secret. Every time I would have to endure the smug advice of another parent toting her sleep-glutted wunderkind, I would think, *I have tried everything possible to fix this problem. If Dr. Ferber can't fix it, then it's unfixable.*

In a weird way, I think this was the outcome I was hoping for. I imagined Ferber working intensely on our daughter, canceling all of his appointments and speaking engagements to direct all of his brilliance toward her. He would let her scream for days in a padded room that he would spray down with Lysol every few hours, but she would persevere. She would be his greatest challenge. A medical anomaly. Never in his thirty years of practice (he would say) had he seen such a child. She must be a genius. How lucky she was to have such patient and insightful parents who had the guts to make that call. But there's nothing to be done. Nothing. (A pause: He removes his glasses and rubs his giant brain-vein.) "I have exhausted all of my expertise, all of my tricks. If I can't make this child sleep through the night, then no one can."

Then he would send us home, vindicated. When people would hear about our vampire child and ask in that patronizing tone, "Well, have you tried Ferberizing her?" we would finally have the iron-clad response: "Why, yes. Yes, we have." Then I'd reach into my impeccably organized diaper bag and pull out the laminated article from the *New England Journal of Medicine* featuring my little genius. Judgment would turn to awe.

Don't get me wrong. There was a part of me that was hoping

it would work, but I liked this story a lot and kept adding to it as the months went by. It kept me warm and safe through that frigid winter.

Then things, as they always do, started to change: Winter turned to spring; I didn't need my Brest Friend anymore; my baby son inexplicably, accidentally really, started sleeping through the night. Even my daughter started waking up just once instead of twice or three times. Sometimes.

In June, I got a call from Dr. Ferber's receptionist to confirm my appointment. And you know what? I didn't think twice before telling her I didn't need it anymore. When I hung up the phone, it took me a few moments to realize the hugeness of what had just happened: I had actually broken up with the man of my dreams.

My daughter's eight now. She's a great kid, but she still usually wakes up at least once a night and calls out for a snuggle or a blanket, or just because she can. We have, according to the books, utterly failed. But when I walked away from my Ferber fantasy, I also walked away from what those books represent: the idea that every child can and must be shaped into the same perfect being, and our need to get the gold star for doing it perfectly and by the book.

Now, instead of lying about how well my family sleeps, I tell people that I canceled on Dr. Ferber. I feel kind of proud about it. Because when I did it, I owned what every parent knows but few of us publicly admit: that this is a sloppy job, and no amount of Lysol can wipe out all the messy, petrifying imperfections it brings out.

Even if the real reason was that I was just too tired to go.

A NEIGHBORLY DAY FOR A BEAUTY

Peter Horton

IN CERTAIN WAYS I TOOK the long way up the mountain. Becoming a father was one of them. There were times where fatherhood might have come earlier. That girl in college, that engagement, that first marriage. Especially that first marriage. I had always assumed I would have children. Taken it for granted. Maybe because I came from a family of one girl and one boy, I always assumed I'd have one of each. Assumed I'd have them early. When I envisioned myself at forty it was always in my father's image. An idealized image. An image frozen in a photograph standing by a cargo ship, looking off at something in the distance, in that forced, posed way as if someone had said, "No, not in the lens, look over there. It makes you look more satisfied with your life." Standing proudly at the beginning of "having it all": a career in shipping, a wife he seemed to adore, and two well-behaved, too shy to really rebel children to climb all over him when he'd get home from work—late at night, or back from various ports: from a two-day trip to Seattle or two weeks to New York or that two and a half months to Hong Kong. The longest two and a half months of my life.

The wall facing my desk has a vertical collection of black-and-white photographs. At the top is Elwood Horton, my great-grandfather, sitting with a collection of other men around a campfire somewhere in the woods of the Northwest.

Right below is Floyd Elwood Horton, my grandfather, arms raised, fists closed: a portrait from his days as an amateur boxer.

Right below that, William Floyd Horton, my father.

Then two imagined spaces, one for me—Peter William Horton—and one for little me whose only name in dispute would be his first.

But forty came and went without children, without the security of the steady career, and with my second marriage but a dot on the horizon. The childhood image of what my life was going to be had cracked, almost to the point of collapse, held in place no longer by romantic illusions of marriage, career, or even my father, who eight years earlier, on his sixty-fourth birthday, had died of an aneurysm in the middle of a tennis game with my mother. A death so sudden and tidy it carries no proof or certification, just hovers like a statistic in my family history.

The one last great hope, the adhesive that still held the fragile image in place, was the prospect of children. If I could just have children, that image would resurrect, re-adhere in some magical way, and my life as imagined would reengage and continue as if the divorce, the death of my father, and my age were but potholes in otherwise smooth asphalt.

"Is that a line?" My wife was standing on the balls of her feet, spine bent forward, that little white wand held carefully as if it were somehow more than a messenger. As if, were it shaken or dropped, like those Magic 8-Balls, it might come up with a different answer. A sparkle, a daring to hope in her eyes as she presented it to me for confirmation.

I leaned cautiously forward, and there it was. A pink line growing stronger in the circular center of what looks more like a kazoo than anything medical. Anything reliable. We immediately called the doctors. "Yes. There are false negatives but not false positives. You're pregnant." That was it. I was in! The clog in the drain officially broke, and every pent-up projection flooded out aggressively in search of hooks to hang from. I immediately started a journal, recording every feeling, every external sign of life, gluing in every ultrasound picture from when she was the size of a peanut to sucking her thumb and gazing out through that X-rayed veil, peaceful, knowing who the mother was but wondering who the other guy, the cheerleader, the one who kept waking her up by singing loudly and off-key to her mother's stomach, was. I had arrived, and I wasn't going to let one detail pass unnoticed and unrecorded.

My friends, the ones who had had kids when you were supposed to, were suddenly giving me that look. The one that says, "Ahhhh. Okay. You're not the aberrant, underdeveloped, object of spinsterly pity we thought you were. You're in. You're one of *us*; the normal ones." All was well with the world. I was gonna be okay after all.

When my daughter was born, all *was* well with the world. In fact, in that moment she was my world. I suppose the long buildup amplified the miracle, and as I spent those first few sleepless nights at the hospital, engaged in the steepest learning curve of diapers, swaddles, and burpies I could've imagined, the floor dropped out from beneath me and filled with water. I was suddenly swimming in depths I didn't know were possible: depths of love, intimacy, and intense devotion. But gradually I also became aware of other currents swirling beneath my feet; currents less romantic: vulnerability, responsibility, even abject terror. Up until that very moment, I had been able to carry that impervious swagger of youth, the one that says, "If the plane crashes I'll just duck under the thermal blowtorch and somehow break out the emergency exit door. Maybe even save some people as I go." But now the stakes had changed. It wasn't just me anymore. I was needed. In fact, a year later, in late September 2001 when the planes were just beginning to fly again, I had to go on a business trip. The night before, my daughter woke and I went in to put her back to sleep. Moments later, to the rhythmic, effortless wheeze of inhales and exhales, she drifted back in, safe, secure. I, however, spent the rest of the night lodged by her bed, terrified, but not for me. As I watched her chest rise and fall, all I could think was, who besides her mother could ever love her, protect her, listen to her like I would? What a tragedy, a true tragedy, if I ever missed watching her grow and become...her. Suddenly I wanted to survive. To stay alive. And that desire, released and struggling to inflate like a fast-falling parachute, revealed the fragility, the danger all around. In that moment I realized the world, for me, had changed. Would never seem the same again. A few years later when that pink line reappeared, I foolishly thought two would somehow dilute the fear, somehow return to me a modicum of my old cocky self. Well, no such luck.

The parallel universe expanded. After the contraptions, creams, powders, baby groups, and new friends (all with children now, as the old friends, the single ones, convinced I had suddenly turned rude and boring, had disappeared), I found a parallel universe on TV. In fact, I found a whole new world of TV: *Caillou*, *Dragon Tales*, *Angelina Ballerina*, and, of course, *Barney*: that right-wing, repressive, puritanical conspiracy to turn our children's natural impulses into some preprocessed, plastic cheeriness better suited for an Up with People reunion tour than anything authentic. Then there's Mr. Rogers. Thank God for Mr. Rogers. You know, as a child I don't think I ever appreciated what an athlete he was. Really. "It's a beautiful day in the neighborhood a beautiful day for a neighbor (jacket off and in the closet) would you be mine (sweater on, zipper up) could you be mine . . ." And this would go on, with eyes focused—not on his nimble feats that involved hangers, zippers, and closet doors, and the grand finale of street shoes off and tennis shoes (laces tied, in double bows!!) on—with eyes focused solely, and with nary a blink, on us. On me. All with the ease of Kobe going for a jam from the top of the key. Talk about your *über*parent.

Then there's music—and this is where I used to really be cool. I learned piano and guitar mainly to get girls. I used to say it was because I loved music so much, but that was really to get girls, too. All throughout my twenties and thirties, that was really the frosting on my cool cake. I mean, not only was I an actor and a director, I was also a musician—with a degree in composition, by the way; which meant I must be a serious musician. I would then proceed to play the only two classical pieces

I could remember from my college days, and that would be that with that. Unless, of course, the woman was into music herself. Then I'd have to admit that it was not actually a degree from a music conservatory but a liberal arts degree in music, and that the two pieces I was playing aren't really that hard to play—in fact, most high-school piano students can play them—and then I'd be revealed for the musical fraud I actually was. And that would be that with that. Now, however, not only have I forgotten the two pieces from college and all the other cool pieces I used to know, I've learned the whole depressing repertoire of *Barney*, been turned on to Raffi, and find myself offended by the drug references in "Puff, the Magic Dragon" which my daughter makes us play over and over and over again. I am now officially no longer cool.

Okay, back to that second pink line in the kazoo. When I found we were having another, once again that tattered and torn childhood image failed me. Instead of that overwhelming rush of unclogged emotion I had felt the first time, I felt guilt. How could I ever love anyone as much as I loved my daughter? How could that little girl who had been the center of our lives for her whole life be expected to move over and share our attention? Where would she ever find the context for that? Then we found out our second child—you know, the one that was supposed to be a boy?—was actually a girl. I just didn't know what to feel. So I decided it was time for another journal. I bought one totally different from the first. Cracked it open, poised my pen, and prepared to write, but nothing came. Weeks went by, and all I had written was "Dear Ruby...hi."

I sang loud and off-key to her mommy's belly again. Except for the nights it took too long to put Lily to bed. Or the nights my wife was too tired. Or the nights I'd just forget.

That summer was a big one for my first daughter. We went abroad, we moved to a new house, and she started preschool all in a space of about three months. All of which made me even more protective, even more guilty about the coming invasion.

Finally, the day of Ruby's birth. I was sure this truly would open the gates, and to a degree it did. When she first came out, screaming to the gods, I walked over to the examining table and started talking to her. She stopped and turned her head toward me. Seemed to really look. I picked her up and brought her to her mommy to nurse for the first time, and my heart expanded. Life gives snow days for death and birth; at least for the first child. No such luck for the second. For the second there would be no sleepovers at the hospital, or hours upon hours to gaze, uninterrupted. Lily still needed to go to school, to playdates, get fed, get put to bed, and she needed to adjust.

The first time Lily picked up Ruby and slammed her to the floor like something out of the World Wrestling Federation, I thought maybe it was an accident. Then I saw the smile on her face and realized my sweet first daughter had become a demon. In fact, my wife and I lovingly refer to this time as her demon phase. She'd accidentally drop a jar of peanuts on the dog, who would run out of the house whimpering. "Oh, poor doggy," I'd say. She'd say, "I did it on purpose." I'd pick her up firmly, say, "I don't like you hitting your sister," and whack, I'd get one upside my head. My memories of sibling torture were things like my older sister dressing me up as the princess so she, dressed as the prince, could dance around me in circles to the music of *Sleeping Beauty*, but I don't remember any body slams or bitch slaps to the head.

Why is it no one tells you two are twice as hard as one? They really are. Two car seats are harder than one. Negotiating who gets the front seat in the double stroller is harder than just plopping one down in one. And in spite of what's advertised, they really do melt down at the same time. They really do lie in bed in the middle of the night and wait until the other has fallen back to sleep before they start screaming. And they are violent little creatures: They break things.

It was about this time I started envying my single friends. You know, the ones who had deserted me earlier for being rude and boring. What's it like, I would wonder, to get up and actually read the newspaper? Not just the headlines but the actual articles? Or just go to a movie or the grocery store without major negotiation, compromise, and manipulation. What's it like to sleep through the night? To go to bed and know that, barring robbers, earthquakes, or drunken neighbors, you will sleep? Sleep *in* even. Or have a day to myself. A day to myself...just like the days I used to have constantly, endlessly, when I was single. Single and dreaming of the day when I'd finally have a wife and kids.

And there, right there in front of me, was a key. Something fundamental, paradoxical, and toxic about human nature: It constantly thwarts its own need for contentment by placing it somewhere other than here. Other than now. I was suddenly reminded of my favorite definition of contentment: wanting what you have. And I wondered, how does one do that? I don't mean in that cheery, Barney way of wanting it because that's what good boys and girls do. I mean really wanting it in that effortless way you want a comedian to be funny, or your team to win another title, or you want to protect your children from harm. Well, I'm still working on that one. I know one thing for sure, though: I've taken refuge over the years in my image of what my life was going to someday become. Well, that refuge has come with a price, a price I'm not willing to pay anymore. And that is my big fat lesson in this life: Life, real life, has nothing to do with images formed in childhood, with preconceptions, projections, or even dreams. Real life unfolds, yes, to a degree through circumstance and choice, but mostly through profound evolution. An evolution we have no real control over. An evolution that drills our deepest and darkest parts with a ruthless bit, but always with love. Always for our goodness.

So the dream, the image, has fully collapsed, and I've come to see that as a blessing. A real blessing. My relationship to my second daughter has arrived. My heart has expanded, all the way. In some ways she's more fortunate than my first. My love for her came clean. Naked. Unencumbered by the dense footlocker scraping across the nursery floor to the foot of my first daughter's crib. Ruby will be blessed by that, although I suspect she will feel cheated out of some of the intensity of being first. I know I did as a child. Although I also remember watching that intensity fester into something unnatural and toxic between my parents and their first. I remember feeling grateful for the distance of being second. My relationship with my first daughter is grand, even though we're having to go through the process of lifting the footlocker out into the alley and away, hopefully before it, too, turns toxic.

And once in a while I can actually feel it. In moments, quiet as a whisper, but there's no denying it. It's here. Living among the details of my life. My life as it is, today. Contentment. And for me, that's enough.

DISCO FEVER

Melanie Hutsell

WHEN OUR SECOND CHILD, LEO, was born, my husband, Fred, put a disco ball in the playroom. This was Fred's attempt to assist me in bringing back the old days in our new phase of life called parenthood. I used to go out dancing three or four times a week. Let me just say that Fred had no intentions of getting his groove on under that disco ball unless it involved doin' the nasty. After we danced the night away at our wedding reception, for him the hunt was over. Mission accomplished. One night when we had a bunch of friends over who were also new parents, I found out they had no desire to dance either. I couldn't believe it! Was Ellen DeGeneres the only person who danced anymore? I did understand a little. I mean, between breast-feeding, changing poopy diapers, and snap-crackle-poppin' our babies into the Baby Björns, who could think about doin' the hustle? Not to mention all the dads who had been blind-sided upon becoming a parent, unable to do anything right in their wives' eyes, therefore not getting any, therefore thinking this would be life as they would know it forever. Was I insane for thinking the disco ball would magically change everything? As people were leaving that night, I found myself standing at the door, beer in hand, yelling out, "Come on, y'all! Fred just turned on the disco ball! Our babies will sleep and we can dance!" My friend Sarah turned and scowled at me. "Are you kidding? My nipples are bleeding." I opted not to press on. After the final guest left, Fred made his usual attempt at sere-nading me with a song he had improvised one foggy day when our daughter Carly was about three months old, "Put that baby to bed! Come on! Let's get busy!" in his best James Brown, which was funny but not a turn-on. I said, "Let's go dance first!" And as always, he said no. Even then, I didn't understand why my desire to celebrate life and feel the freedom of moving my body and dancing was so strong, and other moms didn't feel the same way.

When I went into labor with my firstborn, my platelets went so low that they had to do it the old-fashioned way. They had to put me under or else I could have died. When I came out of the anesthesia, I was in a huge room with lots of people that had been in car accidents, moaning and crying. All I could do was lie there looking at my somewhat deflated belly, thinking, *Wow, there are people in this building, people other than me, who know the sex of my child, what it looks like, how much it weighs.* Finally, the anesthesiologist came to my bedside. "Melanie, you have a beautiful baby girl, seven pounds even, and by the way, when I was trying to get the tubes down your throat—you have a very small mouth"—I thought, *Hey talk to my husband about that. He'll have a bitch session with you—*"I noticed a couple of nodules on your thyroid. You should get them checked out." For the next five weeks I put that little piece of information in the back crevices of my brain and enjoyed my beautiful baby girl, Carly Rose Rapoport. Well sort of. Actually I felt the nodules all the time. It was like, bask in the smells and beauty of my newborn, feel the nodules, change the baby, feel the nodules, feel my boobs, feel the nodules, drink the herbal tea that my massage therapist made for me that tasted like shit but was supposedly going to get rid of the nodules, feel the nodules. Yep, still there.

When Carly was five months old, I went into the hospital to have the nodules removed. When I woke up from this surgery, I was in a single room waiting—only this time alone. Again, *Somebody in this building has the information right now.* I mean, every doctor I had talked to said it was probably nothing, so it was probably nothing, but still. Fred walked in. Without him saying a word, I knew it was bad. He said, "Honey, it's cancer. They removed the nodules and your thyroid, and it actually spread to a few lymph nodes, and they took those out, too." My mind began to race—lymph nodes, Gilda Radner, Debra Winger in *Terms of Endearment*. Had Carly come into my life to save me, or was I going to have a quick visit and have to communicate with her from the other side? Who would raise her? Would Fred fall in love again? Would he go for a Jewish girl this time? It might be easier. Yeah! He should go for the Jewish girl. Maybe he'll find somebody who's more organized. Great. Jerk. Maybe it was all those hot dogs I ate as a kid. I was obsessed with carcinogen-filled hot dogs. That's all I would eat for the longest time. My poor mother. Not only did I eat them, I had tons of hot dog paraphernalia: hot dog necklace, hot dog T-shirt, hot dog joke book. I even had a giant stuffed hot dog that my Aunt Debbie made; the weenie came out of the bun, and I slept with the weenie. I used to run through my yard with a red cape on holding the stuffed weenie like it was some sort of weapon and yell, "Captain Hot Dog comes to save the day!" Yes! A character based on a cancer-causing meat product! That afternoon my mom came to the hospital with Carly. Seeing my mother standing there, trying desperately not to fall apart, holding my baby girl, who was screaming and crying, was too much. I could hardly look at them. Eventually, everybody went home. There I sat, trying to keep my milk up, pumping my boobs like a cow.

That was the longest night of my life. Unable to sleep, I got up to just walk around a bit and caught a glimpse of myself in the mirror. I remember thinking, *Hey, that bright blue bandage totally brings out my eyes! Fuck. I have Cancer."* Just as the sun started seeping through the blinds, the surgeon's assistant walked in, rested, way too energetic.

"Hi, Melanie!"

"Yeah, hi, so am I going to die or what?"

"Ha ha, no, you have happy Cancer."

"Well, thanks a lot for telling Fred that. All we knew all night was that it had spread to the lymph nodes. That's a pretty scary word!"

"Hey! Weren't you on *Saturday Night Live*?"

"Yes."

"What was that like?"

"It was fi— I don't want to talk about this! What's next for me?"

"Well, from here you will stop breast-feeding immediately. You'll have radiation in six weeks. You'll have to be in isolation for ten days, away from Carly."

Didn't that nurse just tell me I have happy Cancer?

I actually did stop breast-feeding for ten days, and then, thank God, I found a doctor who made sense. He told me that I didn't need the radiation, the Cancer was most likely gone, and I should go back to breast-feeding right away. It took ten days of pumping to get the milk back.

It took quite a while for my body to adjust hormonally from having a baby and losing my thyroid. They put me on a drug called Cytomel, and it made me feel like I was a hundred years old but at the same time like I'd had five espressos. My legs and feet ached all the time, and I got tested a lot. Every time I had to wait for another result, I would put Carly in the stroller and go out to shoot hoops behind Venice High School. I would play a game with myself about my future. *If I make it, I live. If I miss, I die.* This was a really bad idea.

Amidst all this craziness, of course, we wanted to share Carly with Fred's family. So we took her to Chicago. When we first got there, it was Fred's great-uncle Helmut's birthday. Uncle Helmut's wife, who was ninety-six, a spry little thing with short gray hair, martini in hand, came up to me and said loudly in front of Fred's entire family, "Did you get the Disney CD I sent Carly? You didn't send a note, no call, no note, no call. We never knew if you got it or not!" I quietly replied, "I guess you haven't heard, I've had a lot going on, but that's really no excuse." I took Carly upstairs and pulled her to my breast to feed her. I was finally crying.

When we returned home to Los Angeles, we were waiting for the biggest result yet. Because of the platelet issue combined with the thyroid Cancer, there was a very outside chance that the Cancer had spread to my bones. I know, what happened to that damned happy Cancer? Of course I was convinced that I would be the one in a million to have thyroid Cancer spread to my bones. I get my pessimism from my dad. Whenever he goes fishing, he always says, "Well, I probably won't catch any." Or when he watches UT football, we could be up by twenty points, "Yeah, we'll probably lose." "Dad, there's only two minutes to go!" "It can be done!" But in the case of my Cancer, I said to him one day, "So, Dad, do you think this is it for me?" fully expecting him to say, "Well, yeah, you'll probably kick the bucket." Instead, he said, "No, babe, no I don't."

Then I got angry. Friends would call me up and say, "How you feelin'?" I would bark back, "Fine! How are you feeling?" Being from the South, of course, I had lots and lots of people praying for me. One teacher that I didn't even know had her entire class send me get-well cards, and I hated it. *Hated* it!

Every night, I would feed Carly like clockwork at 3:00 A.M., and then I would go in the bathroom and pray. "Please, God, don't let this be it. Don't take me out. I have so much to do. Carly needs me. Fred needs me. Please don't let me die. Not now." I would whisper these things over and over and over again until one night it got really intense. I felt like I was losing my mind. I actually heard God speak. I believe that God comes to us in a form that we as individuals can accept. Being an actor and a child of the seventies, of course mine was Charlton Heston's voice from *The Ten Commandments*, blaring inside my head. No matter how fast I paced through my house to get away from the voice, it wasn't going away. But when I finally calmed down enough to listen, he simply said, "Just hold your baby. Just hold your baby." They say never to wake a sleeping baby, but after I heard God speak, I went into my bedroom, picked up my sweet, sweet Carly Rose, and held her till morning. I had never felt so alive.

That very day, I got out all of those get-well cards and read every last one of them and cried like a baby. Within the hour, Fred came home with calcium-enriched Special K and said, "The doctor said you need lots of calcium so maybe this will be good." Then I cried even more. I was finally able to receive the love, the kind of love that people have to give even when they don't know you. I took it all into my heart, and I was grateful. The doctor called and said the Cancer had not spread to my bones. I called my parents right away, and my father answered. He was outside, and as he wept he fell to the ground saying, "Oh thank you Jesus, praise Jesus. Thank you Lord." I wasn't the only one worried I'd be the one in a million.

After everybody left the party that night and Fred and I went our separate ways, I went into the playroom, turned on the song "Pump It," by the Black Eyed Peas, and danced under the disco ball until I sweat, all by myself.

NO HOVERING

Tom Shillue

THE OTHER DAY I WAS shuffling through selections on my daughter's new CD trying to find the song she wanted to hear. "No—uller one!" she kept saying. Why was I doing this? I never ordered my parents to find the proper song to go along with my mood. I never ordered my parents to do anything. I was afraid to speak to my dad until I was twelve, and even then it was only to ask for a "point of clarification" for something he ordered me to do.

Another unsettling thing is that *my daughter has her own CD collection*. And the children's music on these CDs is filled with political ideology. I finally found the song she was looking for, and this is how it went.

Hey na-na, hey na-na. Hey na-na, hey na.
The Earth is our Mother,
We must take care of Her.
The Earth is our Mother.
We must take care of Her.

Agnes is two. Can you at least wait until she is five to indoctrinate her into the Democratic Party? I know she's headed that way; she is growing up in New York City. Just relax a little—you'll get her in time.

I want to give her a little balance. My Manhattan-born friends are all racked with insecurities and neuroses. I grew up in a very conservative home, and I turned out fine. Perhaps there is something to that.

If you've ever read any parenting blogs or magazines, you've probably read about "helicopter parents," parents who are constantly hovering over their children, trying to make sure their world is free from all danger and stress. I don't want to be a helicopter parent. I see them everywhere. Like the parents in Central Park: "Honey, watch out! The grass—it's sharp!" That's right. Sharp grass.

My mother used to tie me to a tree in the backyard. That way, I could play outside unsupervised. I would run around in a fifteen-foot radius to the tree like a dog. I usually stayed taut at the end of the rope, but sometimes I would run around and around, eventually coiling myself tightly to the tree. I'm lucky there were no large birds of prey in Massachusetts—with the rope wrapped tightly around me, I probably looked like one of those roulade roasts Alton Brown prepares on the Food Network. Eventually, a passerby would happen upon me and help me unwind. One day, my mother decided to let me off the leash. Her only instruction: "Don't go in the street." For a while, I went right back to the half-moon-shaped trench I had worn out in front of the tree, where I felt most at home. Then at some point I broke out on my own, completely forgetting my mother's instruction.

My mother came out on the porch when she heard a car horn honking. I was sitting in the middle of the street, there was a big Chrysler in front of me, and the driver was leaning out the window making a "shoo!" gesture with his hands. This apparently callous behavior by the driver was entirely unre-markable—it was the 1970s, and children were by and large seen as pests, not America's most precious resource. As my mother tells it, upon seeing her, I walked up on the porch, where she was standing arms akimbo in the doorway, and passed by her into the house. I returned moments later with the rope and harness and handed it to her.

My mother likes to tell this story, with that image of me handing back my leash as the punch line, an example of my precocious nature. But as a parent now, I think the more illu-minating part of the story is the earlier part—in the setup. *In taking me off the leash, my mother was willing to roll the dice, and see if I lived to tell about it.* You can hardly accuse her of being a helicopter. But there was a lesson to be learned: I would not again go in the street.

What if the experiment did not end well? What if my mother stepped outside to find me lying on the road with a Michelin tire tread across my forehead? What then? Well, there would be a silk purse from that sow's ear as well: She had five kids, and the other four would learn a valuable lesson. You can bet that at my funeral, as my little casket was being lowered into the earth, my mother would turn to my brothers and sisters and say, "Do you see what happens when you go out in the street?"

Bottom line is, this noninterventionist method worked. I turned out fine, as did my siblings. I would like to emulate my parents today, but I can't completely resist the culture at large—after all, this is a world in which gangly preteens still have to ride in car seats. (Have you seen these Baby Huey–like monsters, riding down the highway strapped into a tiny booster, playing Doom on their Sony PSPs? The boy has five o'clock shadow—let him use a seat belt.)

So I put the song on the CD, and even sang along with it, doing the hand gestures with my daughter.

Hey na-na, hey na-na. Hey na-na, hey na.
The Earth is our Mother,
We must take care of Her.
The Earth is our Mother.
We must take care of Her.

I want to give her an alternative to the indoctrination, though. I know she's not going to be raised as I was, but I want to make sure she gets a little balance in her life. So I wrote this, and I read it to her before she goes to bed.

Dear Agnes,
The Earth is not your real mother. Mommy is. You know Mommy . . . she's the one who feeds you, and gets you dressed, and cleans up your throw-up. If you vomit on Mother Earth, it just sits there.

Mother Earth is also completely indifferent to your suffering. Just imagine if you were alone in the woods and you came upon a hyena. Would Mother Earth rise up between you and the hyena to protect you? No. Mother Earth would sit and watch as the hyena ate you. What about Mother Earth's friends, the trees? Would they be willing to help? No. They would stand idly by, their boughs blowing in the breeze, as if this were the most pleasant thing that they had ever seen. "Look—a little girl being devoured by a hyena . . . Sure is windy today."

But your real Mommy and Daddy won't let that happen. That's why we're here. To protect you from her—Mother Earth. Just imagine if Daddy didn't build a house on her to keep you safe. Or go out and hunt pheasant every day to feed you. Or dig underground for fossil fuels to keep you warm. None of which Daddy actually does—but he's somewhere in the chain of command. Goodnight Moon.

So balance, I believe, is the key. Perhaps I'll be able to strike a happy medium—go along with the rest of the world but offer some resistance. I may not be constantly hovering in my helicopter, but I'll be there. More like one of those golf cart security guards who do laps around the parking lot at the mall. I'll keep a lookout as best I can, and if I miss something, I'll be around again in twenty minutes.

YOUR LOUDMOUTH LESBIAN FRIEND

Marcia Wilkie

HEY THERE. HELLO. IT'S ME, your loudmouth lesbian friend.

In our transient society, with so many parents of young children living long distances from their in-laws or know-it-all aunts, it really has fallen on the shoulders of the lesbian community to step up and be the voice of reason for all our straight sisters who have been hormonally altered through childbirth.

Many have lost that most precious commodity: common sense.

Here I am, the voice of reason. You can count on me.

You called me yesterday, seeking a friendly voice, exhausted from being up all night with your feverish two-year-old.

So, I said: "You know, you're destroying your son's immune system giving him antibiotics."

It's what you needed to hear, especially since you've walked the floor for forty-eight hours carrying twenty-four pounds of screaming kid, yanking his ear off his head.

"Listen to me," I said, pleased to have the perfect answer. "Get a pencil and write this down. Ready? Give your baby one teaspoon of crushed garlic mixed in a tablespoon of fish oil. That should resolve the infection."

When you tell me that right now your child spits even cherry-flavored Tylenol back out, I think to myself, *Here's a parent who lacks persistence.* But what I say out loud to you is "You're the adult. Don't allow that."

Raising children is often just that simple. Isn't it?

Yes. It's me, your loudmouth lesbian friend. Though I have never even read a baby book and I spend less than forty-five minutes a month around anyone under eighteen years old, I know that I can tell you exactly how to parent your child. I can mouth off advice for any age, from babyhood to the bachelor's degree.

For example: When your fifteen-year-old comes home from the school dance with a slight smell of beer on her breath, you can count on me to say something useful, like "Wow. That's a big red flag for future problems."

Certainly you needed that warning. Somehow, I imagine you saying to your coparent (if there is one), "You know, our loudmouth lesbian friend might have a point. Perhaps the stocked liquor cabinet we had planned to give our daughter for her Sweet Sixteen isn't such a great idea. And I'm going to return the fake ID we had made for her."

Lucky for you, I'm the loudmouth lesbian friend who is there for you, right from the start.

I show up at the hospital, the day after your C-section, and say comforting things like "Do you think you'll ever regain any muscle tone in your abdomen?" Then I ask to hold your little newbie, bobbling his tiny head around like a Slinky as only a childless lesbian can. Ten minutes later I offer up: "I'd love to stay, but did you know that the fluorescent lighting in hospitals sucks important nutrients out of the human body? Besides, I'm fighting off a killer sore throat." Before leaving, I lean into the baby's bassinet to give him a smooch.

It's obvious you're being dramatic when you tell me with a shaky voice that you're weary and weepy, you love your son, but you're afraid you'll fail as a mom, and that your nipples are sore from trying to breast-feed.

"You'll be okay in a day or two," I reassure.

"Really?" A look of hope breaks through your glazed-over expression.

"Sure," I say. "I'm a dyke. I know a thing or two about sore nipples. They heal."

With that, I'm out the door. I can't be late for happy hour at the Closet.

I DON'T MEAN TO SOUND self-important, but clearly, I had the solution when you called me for advice. I could hear the desperation in your voice.

"The baby has been upset for weeks," you tell me. "Ten hours a day, and it's making me crazy. My pediatrician said its colic."

I try to speak in calming tones as I tell you that the solution is within reach.

"Get a dab of gel, rub it between your palms, and gently pat it into your baby's hair, until the cowlick lies down. There's no reason to get hysterical over a month of bad hair days."

What would you do without your loudmouth lesbian friend? I'm the one who shows up to your five-year-old's birthday party with a bucket of gummi worms, a Super Soaker, and ten cans of Silly String.

The kids have been quietly putting a puzzle together on the floor while the parents chat over coffee and bagels.

I pull you aside. "See, this is why childhood obesity is rampant," I say, pointing to the composed, contented kids.

Two minutes later I have every child running and screeching through your clean house as I make crazy monster noises and chase them with the giant water pistol. It is only after one kid has crashed head-first into a door jamb, corn syrup solids have been drooled across the sofa, and every child is panting and crazed and moments from a meltdown that I announce my departure. It's been fun, but I've got a 3:30 massage.

As a tried-and-true loudmouth lesbian, I'm great at pointing out your parenting shortcomings.

You looked so happy on the afternoon you got an hour away without kids to grab lunch with me, until I noticed a clean diaper in your backpack.

"He's still not potty trained at three and a half?" I shriek, because you just don't have enough shrieking in your life.

"Every child is different," you shrug, going back to your chopped chicken salad.

I, more than many, know that "every child is different." After all, my mother never expected to raise a lesbian daughter who wouldn't give her grandkids. I just was. It was my nature, my spirit, my road to travel, and those things have very little to do with parenting.

But I can't let it be that simple, or that complicated.

So instead, I think to myself, *This mom lacks initiative*, but what I say out loud is "Well, you better force the issue. Having a Diaper Genie in his dorm room is not going to get him dates in college." With that I secure my loudmouth lesbian title.

HOW MANY HUNDREDS OF TIMES will I slap my head in regret over voicing my unneeded and inexperienced opinion? I'm amazed that you still want a loudmouth lesbian friend around. You wanted your child to know gay people, but I'm sure by now you are wishing you had been more selective.

I know the truth. You don't need a loudmouth lesbian friend telling you how to parent. I need you. I need you because I'm not going to be a parent. I need to be around you and your babies, so I can realistically mark the passage of time. Otherwise, I might fool myself into believing that my whole life is ahead of me, because the only change I see is in a mirror. You, however, have the good fortune of seeing through your offspring that the moment is now. That time, like a growing child, can never be recovered.

Please don't let me become one of those homos that treat their pets like children. I don't want to build a cat condo for Snowflake. I'd rather build a sandbox for your son. I don't want to spend five bucks on a dog bakery treat for Buster, when he's obviously just as happy gobbling up horse turds on a hiking trail. I'd rather buy cookies from your little girl's Scout troop.

Don't let me frame photos of golden retrievers and tuxedo cats. I'd rather show off your child's artwork.

It makes me happy if you need me, too. Because I will be the loudmouth lesbian in the bleachers, cheering on your little cheerleader. I'll glow with pride when your son takes honors at the debate tournament. I'll locate the perfect Halloween costume when their requests are impossible. I'll try to keep your toddler amused with stories and songs when we are stuck in traffic on the I-10 freeway.

Perhaps I'll be the person your child confides in when she feels different, alone, outside of the group, because she will know that I truly understand what that feels like. Hopefully I'll be the one your high school student calls at midnight when she is in the next city at a forbidden party that has turned dangerous and she is too scared to call you to come get her.

I will go to get her, no questions asked. I'll drop her off a half block from your house so you don't see my car. I won't drive off until she's safely through your front door. You will never, ever know about it.

See, I don't always have to be your loudmouth lesbian friend. As your friend, I know that what matters to you most is that your child has another reliable adult in her life: one who would rescue her, no matter what. You can count on me.

A GIRL, A DAD, A GORILLA HEAD:
A CAUTIONARY TALE

Christopher Noxon

SHE WAS JUST SO CUTE, tucked into bed in her favorite purple pajamas, her drowsy eyes and raspy voice sure signs that the fight had gone out of her and we'd arrived at last at the loveliest time of day: actual bedtime.

There was just one problem, one thing keeping my dear five-year-old daughter from ten hours of blissful, silent slumber. Eliza had the hiccups.

Later, what I did next would be subject to considerable scrutiny. Reasonable adults would question my motives. My wife, for one, would wonder what the hell I was thinking. To which I now respond: You should have heard those hiccups. They were like the calls of an impossibly beautiful songbird. They were sweet little peeps. Their sweetness made me stupid.

Of course, I tried the usual remedies first. I coached my daughter on the holding of breath and the counting to ten. I fetched her a spoonful of sugar. I helped her stand on her head. Alas, nothing seemed to work. The hiccups kept coming.

So I devised a plan. It was, admittedly, a dramatic course of action—but it was also, I believed, an original solution to a common problem, one that would affirm my place as both rock-solid protector and freethinking fun guy.

I kissed Eliza good night, stepped into my room, and put on the head of a gorilla suit I happen to own (don't ask). Then, with a vicious roar that was unexpectedly deepened and amplified inside my big rubber mask, I leaped back into her doorway and thumped my chest spastically.

Apparently, I am a very convincing gorilla. When I pulled off the head, Eliza was hiding behind a stuffed kitty cat, her face frozen in an expression of abject terror. Then came the sobbing. And the cries of "Why, Daddy, why?"

This was, without a doubt, a parental low point. The fit subsided soon enough, and Eliza was back to her sunny self the next day, but I couldn't help worrying about long-term trauma. What were the signs of post-gorilla stress disorder? Would my daughter spend years in therapy discussing trust issues because her dad thought hiccups could be cured by a bellowing ape-man in flannel pajamas?

One thing seemed clear: This was not to be discussed outside the immediate family. While I couldn't hide my stupidity from my wife, I hated to think what would happen if this tale entered the Mommy and Me/playgroup chatter. In my mind, such talk was still dominated by type-A perfectionists who earned points trading notes on babyproofing and breast-feeding and otherwise marveling at their triumphs in Raising the

Perfect Child. These parents might admit to the occasional slipup, but I'd never heard anything more serious than missing a bedtime in an all-important sleep schedule or inadvertently giving Junior a corn chip containing partially hydrogenated oil.

I couldn't help myself, though. I had to unburden myself. At a barbecue a few days later, I nervously retold the story for a few fellow harried urban dads. To my surprise, it prompted what I can only describe as a game of Bad Dad One-Upsmanship. One dad got big laughs recounting how he nearly gave his daughter a concussion carrying her on his shoulders through a doorway. Another confessed to leaving his toddler strapped into a car seat for two hours during a school basketball game.

Over the next few weeks I retold the story every chance I got. By now every parent, nanny, and birthday party clown within a twenty-mile radius knows about the dumb dad in the gorilla head. In return I've been told about many more hair-raising mistakes, misdeeds, and misgivings. (Note to self: Never put diaper cream on a kid's toothbrush.)

All of which might only suggest that I travel in a particularly bad crowd of breeders. But a quick survey reveals an entire industry of parental inferiority. New "momoirs" are filled with tales of overflowing diapers, supermarket tantrums, and sexless marriages, each a supposedly more intimate exposé of the ugly underbelly of parenthood than the last. The titles say it all: *Mommies Who Drink*; *I Was a Really Good Mom Before I Had Kids*; *Sippy Cups Are Not for Chardonnay*. Online, "new parenting" Web sites like Babble.com and Offsprung.com post blogs like "Terrible Mother" and "Bad Parent."

At its worst, this sort of warts-and-all disclosure is a sly and insensitive shtick, a self-conscious exercise for reluctant adults to ease the guilt about failing to live up to our responsibilities.

But I'm here to tell you, there's nothing like hearing about another parent's failings to make you feel better about yourself: *I may have terrified my daughter with a gorilla head, but at least I never left her strapped in the car seat for two hours.*

It's not as if I'm oblivious to the joys of parenthood. I'm always the first dad to whip out my family portrait, mostly because I take enormous pride in my kids. But I also get a kick out of explaining how we forgot the diaper bag that particular night and how my youngest son took a big dump the moment before the picture was taken. And that episode with the gorilla? My daughter may have been traumatized, but I'm here to tell you: She hasn't had the hiccups since.

HITLER'S LOVE CHILD

Deborah Copaken Kogan

I FORCE MY SCREAMING TWO-YEAR-OLD into his car seat, wedging my knee into his groin for leverage. Paul, my husband, has to work this weekend, so it's just me and the terrorist on a two-day journey from New York City to Freedom, Maine. My eldest, Jacob, thirteen, is starring in his camp production of *Little Shop of Horrors*, and he's written us a passive-aggressive letter saying he knows we weren't planning on visiting this year—his father and I have dutifully made the journey to camp now four years in a row—but wouldn't it be great if one of us could be there to see the show?

"You're insane," said my husband. "How are you going to drive twelve hours, by yourself, with a two-year-old?"

"Easy," I said. I reminded him that I once spent several

weeks packed cheek-to-jowl with Afghan soldiers in the back of an open truck as snow and Soviet bombs fell from the sky; that I found my way in and out of the jungles of Zimbabwe, alone and without compass or vehicle; that I drove across the continent of Europe in a twenty-year-old jalopy with my psychopathic Romanian boyfriend *after* we'd broken up. How hard could it be to drive a toddler to Freedom?

"Crackers! Crackers! Crackers!" screams Leo, with the same intensity as someone having his nails extracted with pliers.

I'm prepared for this moment. I've worked my whole life toward this moment. From a shopping bag, I pull out a gigantic box of Pepperidge Farm Goldfish crackers, bigger than the kid himself. "Is your mommy great or what?" I say, shaking the container, seeing my son's eyes widen with awe. Then silence—glorious silence—fills the car.

WHEN PEOPLE ASK, AS THEY inevitably do, what on earth we were thinking when we decided to have baby Leo, nine and eleven years after his older siblings, we tailor the answer to our audience. To our friends dealing with infertility, we shrug our shoulders and change the subject or make some lame joke about being gluttons for punishment. The childless by choice get the whole "He was an accident." Our parents think he was planned. Our big kids think we had him to avoid getting a dog.

It's not that we get off on lying—at least no more than the average kindergartner—it's just that the real story takes too long to tell. Plus, frankly? It's a little embarrassing.

Birth control and I have had a rocky history. I got knocked up at seventeen using a diaphragm. (Thank you, Planned Parenthood, for helping me out of that one. This year's donation is in the mail, earmarked for Bristol Palin.) I went on the pill after that, and then, after giving birth to my eldest two, I got an IUD so I'd never have to think about birth control again.

Imagine my surprise, then, when, three years later, I found myself surrounded by a dozen ultrasound technicians and technicians-in-training, all of whom were called in to check out the freak show in room ten. "See," said my technician, thrusting the prophylactic-covered wand deeper inside me and pointing to the distinct T-shaped shadow on the screen, "There's the intrauterine device"—she then pointed to a blob— "and that's the embryonic sac." Audible wows could be heard, in stereo, but I was too busy gasping for air and thinking about the oral toenail fungus medication I'd been taking for over a month, the one with the label warning, in big red letters, CONTRAINDICATED FOR PREGNANCY.

"You can have this baby," said my OB the next day, "but it probably won't resemble any life form you're used to seeing, assuming it's not stillborn."

"Poor Gimpy," said my husband, trying to make me laugh, contorting his hands and face into a monstrous creature and mimicking the voice of Lenny in *Of Mice and Men*. "Help! Help! I've got an IUD stuck in my eyeball!"

We scheduled the D and C for the following week and carried on with our lives.

I went on the patch after that, but the increased hormones caused a third breast to sprout under my armpit. Compared to the cancerous tumor my doctor originally feared it might be, I didn't mind my mutant breast so much, but still. "Maybe you should lay off the estrogen for a little while," I was told, and suddenly I was back to my trusty old friend from high school, the diaphragm.

I broached the idea of a vasectomy with Paul, and he started ranting about Hitler. "What about our third kid?" he said, even though we'd planned to have just two. "We have to replace the Jews lost in the Holocaust."

"That's ridiculous," I said. "I'm not having a third kid to spite Hitler."

"It's not about Hitler. It's about the *dead Jews*."

"Well, I'm not having a third kid for them either. Plus, let's get real," I said. Though both of us were working full-time, guess which one of us had yet to meet the pediatrician or pick nits out of his children's scalps?

My husband promised to be more present. He began Freudian analysis to deal with his baggage: the father who'd abandoned him at birth; the mother who died when he was fifteen; the adoptive parents who'd survived the Holocaust. He took over cooking, bill paying, food procurement, and even the occasional pediatrician appointment. He began coming home from work in time for dinner. "So," he said one evening, during this era of reformation. "What do you say about that third kid?"

"No," I said. "We've got a great family the way it is now."

This debate went on for years, back and forth, back and forth, until finally, late one night when I was thirty-nine, and the window of opportunity was about to close, Paul came home from a business trip to L.A., woke me up from a deep slumber, and made such a passionate, plagiarized plea for a third child—"If not now, when?"—I calculated where I was in my cycle (safe, I was certain) and left the diaphragm in the drawer. *Let him have this one night of false hope*, I thought. *We'll have a rational discussion about it in the morning.*

Nine months later, despite assiduous use of the diaphragm during the rest of that month, Leo was born.

"UH-OH," I HEAR FROM THE backseat, followed by another fingernails-extracted-with-pliers wail, then: "Crackers! Crackers! Crackers!" I look into the rearview mirror to assess the damage. My son is holding the gigantic Pepperidge Farm box upside down, peering into the void for the Goldfish that are now dumped all over the floor of the backseat as if on the deck of a trawler. He starts to scream and thrash, causing his blankie, which he calls "wadi"—as in the Arabic word for valley, which we take as a sign of his support for the Israeli Labor Party—to fall out of his car seat as well.

I pull over to the shoulder and put on my hazard lights once again.

Without boring you with the details, suffice it to say that, about halfway into our journey in the Little Car of Horrors, I am reduced to playing the Herman's Hermits song "I'm Henry VIII, I Am" on automatic repeat, for four hours straight, just to placate the terrorist. "Again! Again!" shouts Leo, when I try to vary the musical fare, and it becomes a philosophical question of the lesser of two evils: Which is worse, a child's ear-splitting screams or "I'm He-ne-ry the Eighth I am, He-ne-ry the Eighth I am, I am..." I'm not saying I chose the right answer, only that I chose *an* answer, which means that now, every time I hear that song, I have a Pavlovian response to it that rivals Alex's to Beethoven's Ninth, post aversion therapy, in *A Clockwork Orange.*

WE FINALLY ARRIVE IN FREEDOM, which truly feels at this moment like just another word for nothing left to lose, on the afternoon of the second day, both of us frazzled and exhausted. Though it's taken us a few extra hours, due to multiple stops along the shoulder of I-95 to retrieve wadi or a fallen cookie or to mop up the apple juice from Leo's lap, we still have plenty of time to spare before the show begins, so after hugging my big kids and taking a tour of the glassblowing shack—during which I ponder whether blowtorches and dry wood have any business commingling—I immediately set out to find a place for Leo to nap, so he won't cause a ruckus during the performance.

We decide to use my daughter Sasha's bed in her cabin, but just as the baby's drifting off to sleep, Sasha's counselor walks over to talk to us. "I'm sorry," she says. "He can't sleep here. It wouldn't be fair to the rest of the girls."

I have no idea what this means. "Fair?" I say. "How so?"

"Their parents aren't here. They might get homesick," she says.

Sasha's been coming to this camp since she was seven years old. She's now eleven. Her bunkmates have been coming since they were eight or nine. They're now twelve and thirteen.

I explain to the counselor, in the most nonconfrontational language I can muster, that I've been traveling for two days, just to see my son's performance. That the baby needs a place to sleep or I won't be able to make this happen.

"You could go find a nice, shady place under a tree or something," she says.

I silently, uncharitably curse her future motherhood, hoping some humorless camp counselor in her early twenties tells her to put her toddler down for a nap on dirt after she's driven with him for two days. "That only happens in paintings," I say. "Two-year-olds don't actually fall asleep under trees in real life. You sure I can't just let him sleep here?"

"I'm sure," she says.

So I wake up my toddler and carry his now exhausted and overstimulated body to the infirmary, where I convince the camp nurse to allow Leo to fall asleep in one of her sickbeds—so what if the last kid in it had strep?—and he takes a full two-hour nap.

The musical is scheduled to begin at 7:00 P.M. in the red barn. Sasha, Leo, and I arrive fifteen minutes early to stake out our spot. Leo is in a great mood, having slept adequately and eaten a proper dinner of chicken and corn, and I'm congratulating myself on having weathered the journey and made it to this moment. Yes, it was more arduous than covering the Soviet retreat from Afghanistan, but *I'm here*, damn it. I showed up. My dad, a former international lawyer at a white-shoe D.C. firm, once interrupted a complicated legal negotiation with the government of the Marshall Islands to fly all the way back to Maryland to see me perform in my sixth-grade play. I've never forgotten that gesture. In fact, of all the sacrifices my parents ever made, this is the one that stands out the tallest.

Other parents of young thespians start arriving in the barn, too, and we smile at one another and nod knowingly—*long trip*, our faces and rumpled clothes say, *but it was worth it*—and wait for the performance to begin. The lights dim. My daughter grabs my hand. My two-year-old settles in my lap, sitting perfectly still. My teenage son steps out onto the stage, owning it. I'm as proud as a parent is authorized to be.

Then, suddenly, Leo breaks the fourth wall. "Jacob! Jacob! Hi! Hi, Jacob!" he starts to shout, standing up in my lap and waving maniacally to his big brother onstage. Jacob tries to ignore him, but it's hard. The audience twitters. The other parents, some of whom have driven longer distances than I, shoot me irritated sneers. Jacob himself shoots me a pleading look: *Control him.* "Jacob! Jacob! Hi!" Leo yells again, his tone now desperate. My path to the door, which had been clear before the campers descended upon the barn, is now completely blocked by young audience members crammed one next to the other on the floor. *"JA-COB! Hi! Hi! Hiiiiiiiiiiiiiiiiiii!!!!!!!!"*

I try reasoning with my two-year-old. When that doesn't work, I resort to threats. "Be quiet," I whisper, "or you won't get any ice cream after the show."

"Ice cream! Ice cream!" Leo shouts. "Outside! Outside now! Hi, Jacob! Hi!" He's still trying to catch his brother's eye. *"Ja! cob! Hi!"*

The other parents in the room now clearly hate me. They glare at me and roll their collective eyes. *What business does she have bringing a two-year-old to a performance?* their pursed mouths ask. *Does she realize how long it took us to get here? For that matter, what business does she have having one in diapers while the other two are going through adolescence? What's wrong with her? What was she thinking?* Okay, so maybe I'm just projecting those last thoughts, since they're the secret ones I sometimes harbor.

"It's Hitler's fault!" I want to shout, but instead I simply stand up and drag my kicking, screaming replacement Jew through the Red Sea of young campers, stepping on fingers, toes, and the occasional water bottle and flashlight, until I reach the door of the barn, and when I get there I realize I've left the diaper bag back at my seat.

Leo, now sprung from the hot and stuffy barn, is positively gleeful, completely forgetting his older brother's slight, dipping the tip of wadi into mud puddles and picking up rocks and weeds and scraps of paper and an old bottle cap and anything

else he finds in his field of vision. I try to stand at the door of
the barn, half in, half out, so I can keep an eye on both kids, but
I soon realize that this is impossible. Just as I turn my back on
the baby to hear Jacob belt out "Suddenly Seymour!" Leo falls
into a mud puddle, chest first, and starts to bawl.

The kid is completely caked in mud, from his hair down to
his sneakers, and I definitely smell something malodorous in
his diaper, but what really bothers Leo is that his wadi is now
soaked. Wadis, apparently, are no good if they're not dry and
soft. Wet, and they might as well be porcupines. So he runs
over and hugs me for comfort instead, and soon I'm covered in
mud, too, and the audience starts to clap, and the play is over.

It's over.

I feel like crying. I feel like screaming. I feel like throwing
myself on the ground and having a Leo-style tantrum. I still
have another hour or so of driving east on poorly marked country roads, in the dark, to a friend's house, where I'll sleep for
the night, then I have to wake up the next morning, wrangle
Leo back into his car seat, and drive the ten/twelve/fourteen
hours back, however long it takes us, to get the rental car back
before 10:00 P.M., so I don't have to pay for the extra day: all
this, for a musical I never even got to see.

"I'm so sorry," I say to my eldest, when it's time to leave.

"It's okay," says Jacob, ruffling Leo's hair. "He's two. He
doesn't know any better."

"Hi, Jacob!" says Leo, waving maniacally again.

"Hi, Leo!" says Jacob, hoisting his little brother into his
arms and smothering him with kisses.

"I know it's okay," I say, "but I came all this way and missed
the whole thing."

"True." Jacob shrugs. Smiles. Puts his brother on the ground and throws an arm around me for comfort, the way I used to when he'd fall into mud puddles as a toddler. "But you came. And I appreciate it." He wrinkles his nose. "Ugh, what's that smell!"

"Oh, yeah, sorry about that. Sasha has the diaper bag." I pick up Leo and search the crowd for my daughter and the diapers. "Hey, you want to go get some ice cream?" I say. "We can go to that same place we went last year."

"Nah, that's okay," says Jacob. "I think I'm just going to stay here and chill with my friends. You're not mad, are you?"

"Of course I'm not mad!" I say, without adding the obvious: *I'm just sad. Profoundly, desperately sad.* My eldest, the bar mitz-vah boy—it suddenly hits me hard—doesn't need me anymore.

"Ice cream?" says Leo, holding my face in his muddy hands for added emphasis. "Ice cream! Ice cream!"

"Okay!" I say, kissing his mud-caked nose, his needy, stinky, tantrum-throwing, glorious toddler self. "Let's go find your sister and get some ice cream!" And as my baby hugs me back, nuzzling his filthy cheek into the crook of my neck, I silently throw a shout-out to whichever kid from Warsaw he's replaced.

AUNT CUCKOO

Dan Bucatinsky

WHAT'S THE EXPRESSION? "CAREFUL WHO your friends are." Is
that it? Or "With friends like these, who needs enemies?" No.
"Keep your friends close—and your enemies closer." Right.
That's not a problem since I'm my own worst enemy. But what
happens when your friends are your enemies? And if your
kids become friends with your friends who are your enemies—
does that make your kid your enemy? I'm getting ahead of myself. . . .

I met my friend Lucy—not her real name—the same night I
met my boyfriend, Don. She had been his assistant for years,
and when I came into the picture, she befriended me. She
was sort of working the grunge thing before anyone else
was—and kept up the trend way past its expiration date. Jet-

black hair, combat boots. And she wore lots of hats. It didn't take long for Lucy and me to become close. We talked every day, laughed, gossiped. Dozens of meals, sometimes with Don, sometimes not.

A few years later, Lucy fell into a sort of depression. She retreated, closed herself off, and put on a lot of weight. Nightmare, right? Why is it you add "put on a lot of weight" to any story and instantly it becomes far, *far* more tragic? Where was I? Right. Big depression. Never left her house anymore—except on occasion, she'd agree to meet somewhere she wouldn't run into anyone she knew. I kept wanting to suggest we meet at Jenny Craig—kill two birds with one stone—but Don thought that might be a little obvious.

After one of these clandestine dinners with Lucy at a Sizzler somewhere deep in the Valley, I told her the good news: Don and I were thinking of adopting! Now, there's a reason people like being bearers of good news. The response is always predictably great: a squeal of delight, a big hug, a hip-hip-hooray . . . or not.

I don't know why I didn't see it coming. No, in the case of Lucy's reaction—Lucy distinguished herself from everyone else we'd told, with all their time-worn, conventional, almost clichéd expressions of enthusiasm: *She tried to talk me out of it.*

Here are some highlights from Lucy's many, many persuasive arguments: "Your life will never be the same." "You'll never sleep soundly again." "You can kiss your relationship good-bye." "Do you know how fast people age once they have kids?" "Old and fat. Get used to those words." (That one almost did it for me.) "You don't have a house for kids: Your floors are limestone. Your stairs are treacherous. Your pool is basically a baby tar pit. Try recovering from a dead baby." Then, as though she saw a tiny bit of life in my still and lifeless body—one more bullet: "And it's not just babies who die. You know how many people die during childbirth?" I managed to croak out, "Um, we're adopting?" She was obstinate: "Google it. But don't let me stop you—maybe you *want* to live with the blood of a child on your hands." I didn't quite know what to say. I just started laughing. Nervously. The way you laugh when you think, *Oh dear, am I in a car miles from anywhere with a crazy person—in what will one day become an urban legend, told by fright-seeking campers in the middle of the night?*

When I got home, I had time to reflect on our conversation—and I got mad. Really mad. How dare she? How dare she try to freak us out? How dare Lucy dissuade us from providing a home for a defenseless child? How dare she reduce me to the kind of guy who says "How dare she?" What kind of person does this to a so-called friend? An enemy. That's what kind. Not in the classical Hezbollah sense of the word—more of a "frenemy"—you know, the kind you love to hate. Or love *and* hate. There's no question I was pissed. But soon my anger turned to sadness. . . . I may be a little bitchy but I'm not cruel, for God's sake. Obviously, she so desperately didn't want us to complete this little family portrait because it felt like we'd be slamming the door on some unconscious dream of her being in that picture—or a picture of her own.

Fast-forward two years. We had decided to adopt. Easy, breezy. Found a lawyer, wrote birth mother letters describing ourselves as we might an airline: "Comfy, entertaining, committed to safety . . . Fly with us!" Then we meet birth mom one, who we discover is doing crystal meth. . . . Easy, breezy. Then birth mom two, from Wisconsin. Help her get her kids back from their father who kidnapped them while running from the law. Easy, breezy. And boom: Four months later, Eliza Rose was born. Contact with Lucy during this period of time was limited at best. Two short visits to see the baby. One with a gift: a stuffed animal, a pink elephant in disco pants—seriously— which I took as a dig. And that was it. Until our daughter, Eliza, was eighteen months old and Lucy found out Eliza was having a heart procedure.

Lucy came out of hibernation to come to the hospital. She was there all day. Before the four-hour operation, during, and after. So when Eliza made a full recovery, I thought, *Okay. Fine. She gets some points. But let's see if she shows up now that the crisis is over.*

She did . . . around once a week to spend time with Eliza. It was awkward at first. Lucy was clunky. And loud. As though Eliza's problem were with her hearing not her heart—no concept of an "inside voice." She'd whip Eliza around in the air, and even though the doctors said it was fine, we weren't so much into the roughhousing right after a heart surgery. We liked smooth-housing or no-housing. Like, "Hey, Eliza? You know what would be fun? Let's sit very still and try to hear heartbeats. *Your* heartbeat, actually. Do you have a heartbeat, darling? Please say yes." But that wasn't how Lucy played it. It was more of a manic BOZO-THE-CLOWN-I'M-FINALLY-OUT- AFTER-BEING-COOPED-UP-FOR-THREE-YEARS-AND- WANT-TO-PROVE-TO-YOUR-DADS-HOW-GREAT- A-MOTHER-I-WOULD'VE-BEEN-IF-THEY'D-HAD-A-BABY- WITH-ME kind of energy. We were sure Eliza wouldn't like it. It was too much for such a delicate little flower.

But Eliza loved it. Was it just that we had a real-life Barney playing with our daughter—and not just when Lucy wore purple? Or was it something else? I snuck in on them once eating cookies out of a box. She whispered, "We don't have to tell Papi or Daddy about every cookie we eat, do we?" *Yes you do!* So, it's the sugar. I knew it. Add that to the TV! I walked in on them on the couch watching what looked like a marathon of commercials for, I don't know, liquor, guns, and Froot Loops. When Eliza was with Lucy there were no rules, no bedtime, no limits. Lucy was her irresistibly wild-eyed, energetic, and fun-loving aunt. Aunt Cuckoo.

And now, eighteen months after Eliza's operation, we are Aunt Cuckoo's bitches. Every morning when we drive Eliza to school she starts asking to call Lucy as we back down the driveway. I dial her on speakerphone. It rings. Eliza's face beams with anticipation. It rings again. No answer. I start to panic—has Lucy passed out, Mama Cass style, after an all-night *Law & Order* marathon, her face buried in a pizza box? *Ring. Ring.* How am I going to explain this to Eliza? *Ring. Ring.* Pick up the phone, Aunt Cuckoo! Eliza looks worried. Then the click— "Hello?" I can breathe again. Eliza smiles. "Hi," she says, suddenly shy—as though she were talking to a celebrity. The pope. Or better, Anderson Cooper. And they talk. Lucy starts: "It's peanut butter jelly time!" Eliza laughs. It's the highlight of her day. And I can't help but resent Aunt Cuckoo for it. I work so hard to provide for my daughter, to teach her about kindness and moderation and limits. Why doesn't she like me, her own father, better than our friend, an unabashed, hedonistic sugar and TV pusher?

I'm embarrassed to admit it, but I try to imitate Aunt Cuckoo sometimes. "Peanut butter jelly time!" Eliza just looks at me—a look I've seen countless casting directors give me. A look that says, "Aww. Nice try, but we're gonna go a different way."

Bedtime's the same. I pick up a book. Eliza just says, "Call

Lucy?" I think: *No way! It's time to cuddle and bond and read.*
"No, sweetie. Aunt Lucy is—is—well . . . " *Can I do it? No. Don't do
it.* "Lucy is sick. Very sick." *Oh, no. I've hit an all-time low. Sick?
You really want to be* that *guy?* I correct myself. "I mean, tired,
sweetie. She's sleeping—which is what you should be doing." I
distract her with some tickling and an organic, all-natural,
high-fiber gummi bear (evaporated cane juice, in case you
were wondering), and we enjoy the last moments before sleep.
"Sweet dreams, monkey. Tomorrow morning, Daddy is going to
make pancakes in little animal shapes and—" She cuts me off.
"Call Lucy?" "Yes! Fine. Tomorrow you can call Lucy." I turn
out the light and slip away, knowing full well she never re-
members anything we talk about right before bed.

Next morning, I look in on my sleeping angel. Her eyes peek
open, *bink*—"Call Lucy?" *For the love of God.* What about Daddy's
pancakes, huh? *What about Daddy's fucking pancakes in the shape
of Daddy's BROKEN HEART?!*

How did it happen? My daughter's a crazy, stalky fan of the
one person who did everything in her power to talk me out of
having her in the first place.

Don't get me wrong: Don and I love Lucy—but it's been a
troubled and troubling relationship, to say the least. Endless
one-sided attempts to connect, all falling on deaf ears. But
Eliza doesn't know that. And she never will, if we can help it.

Because lately I've started to think about how much Eliza's
done for Aunt Cuckoo. She's done what we could never do:
made her feel important, and laugh and run and forget herself, at least for the amount of time it takes to get through five
episodes of *Little Einstein* and a dozen chocolate-chip-and-
hydrogenated-oil cookies. But there it is. I didn't do that. No.
What I did was turn Lucy into my enemy. Why? I don't know.

Probably fear. And Lucy didn't want us to have kids, also because of fear—of change. She wanted to be able to control all the variables. Sound familiar? Didn't someone once say, "Enemies are only mirrors of ourselves"? Well, they should've. Because, like Lucy, I want life to be neat and predictable and safe and calm and quiet and controlled, with *no* surprises, like tricky little heart defects.

I thought Lucy was the enemy because I was afraid. Afraid Eliza would somehow pick Lucy over me—in some larger sense. Eliza herself proved how small and wrong and petty that thinking is. Eliza's big, open, generous heart continues to amaze us with its limitless capacity to accept and love. Who knew? After all this time—it was Daddy who had the heart defect, not Eliza.

So my daughter teaches me what Aunt Cuckoo teaches her. That life is crazy and unpredictable and undisciplined and fundamentally bad for your health, and the sooner you get an Aunt Cuckoo in your life to show you that, the better.

THE LONG HUG

Joan Rater

THE FIRST TIME SALLY LOOKED at me, *really* looked at me, was in the bathtub in our hotel room the day before we left China. She'd spent every waking moment of the two weeks since we'd gotten her—on her first birthday, incidentally—crying. Into space, because not looking at me, or my husband, Tony, or our seven-year-old daughter, Maggie, was, besides crying, the activity that took up all of Sally's day.

At first we took the crying in stride; we were prepared for it, even happy about it—it means she was attached to her caregivers in the orphanage, this is normal, she's shocked, she's grieving, she's . . . she's still crying. After all the other babies in our travel group had stopped crying and started smiling and giggling and delighting their families, Sally continued her wailing. "She's strong-willed," I told Maggie, who had begun her own crying campaign. "That's a good thing, it means she's a fighter, a survivor. Trust me, this is all going to turn out okay." I don't know what was worse, the baby not looking at me or Maggie's worried, watchful gaze. On the outside I was still calm, motherly, putting on a great show for Tony, Maggie, our travel mates, the Chinese people. *I am her mother and I love her.* But inside I was in a panic. *I love her in theory. I'll learn to love her, I'm sure. But right now I don't even like her.*

Seeing the other children in the group blossoming only made it worse. Overheard snippets of parental wonder—"Emily loves to be tickled" or "Look at Maya jangle those keys" or "You should hear Naomi crack up in the bathtub"—would send me into a tailspin. I'd rush back to our room to tickle and jangle. No such luck.

The stress of spending two weeks in China sharing a hotel room with a crying baby, not to mention the accumulated stress of the year we spent waiting and planning this trip, had taken its toll on us all. On a trip to the Guangzhou Zoo, Maggie saw a dalmatian in a filthy cage and literally sank to her knees in despair. "They have a dog in a zoo, Mom. I don't like China. I want to go home." Tony took her home a few days early and left Sally and me to endure the fifteen-hour plane ride together. It was the night before our flight and we were taking a bath. And yeah, she was crying. I took her hands. Look, Sal, splashy splashy splash. I took her feet. Splashy splashy splash. I turned her toward me and started splashing the water with my own hands. Look, Sal, look at Mama, Mama likes to splash, see? Splashy splash splash? My baby was sobbing, and now I was, too. This isn't how this was supposed to go. When I had imagined our trip to China there were no tears. Just smiles and cute dresses and chicken and broccoli in garlic sauce. Not pickled fish and relentless rejection. I took Sally's little crying face in my hands and let loose two weeks' worth of fear and frustration: *"Stop fucking crying!"* I yelled. *"Just fucking stop!!!"* And she did. I know she was just startled, but I like to think she sensed that something important had happened. The white-haired lady with the fake frozen smile who'd spent the past two weeks chirping baby talk—in English, no less—had finally cut the crap and had an honest emotion. Sally looked into my eyes and stayed there. Relief filled the bathtub, splashy splash splashing through my body. I thought, *We've started, we're on our way, we're going to be okay.*

TWO YEARS LATER. THE CRYING has stopped. Sally has learned to walk and talk. She has hit all her developmental milestones. She's smart and funny and so beautiful it takes your breath away. She loves to swim and play, and there are moments, many moments where everything seems normal, good even. And yet . . .

"Mommy, what's that in your hair?"

"A ponytail, Sal."

"I don't like it."

"Well, I do, it keeps the hair out of my face."

"Take it out."

"No, I'm going to keep it in."

"Take it out take it out take it out!!!" She's on the ground now, banging her head against the floor. I take out the ponytail and she stops.

Now, I know all about the terrible twos, threes, and fours. I know how to set limits. I'm not a pushover. I've already raised one toddler through to girlhood. I have no problem giving a time-out, turning a deaf ear to a tantrum. I have watched *Supernanny*. But this is different.

It's dinnertime.

"Mommy, what's your favorite color?"

"Blue, Sally."

"Daddy? What's your favorite color?"

"Red."

"Maggie?"

"Green."

This is the only conversation we have these days. Besides what's your favorite shape and who's your favorite *Sesame Street* character. And it's not a conversation so much as a recitation of the prescribed answers to Sally's questions. For instance—the first time Sally asked me who my favorite *Sesame Street* character was, I said Cookie Monster. Now that's my answer. If I try to change it, Sally cries. If I give two answers, say, Cookie Monster and Big Bird, she sobs. If I refuse to play, she whines until I give in. So I answer—Cookie Monster, Sal. We all do. It's easier. Tony, Maggie, and I push food around our plates and answer triangle or square when asked our favorite shape, which we are over and over again. We're worn down. We fight back every now and then, find a therapist who suggests we buy a dollhouse and do play therapy. Our doll selves get beaten down, too. I spend a few weeks trying to M&M-train Sally to let us talk about other things, to let us talk to each other instead of parroting lines from a boring quiz show. It doesn't go well. We start to have friends come over after Sally is asleep because the bossiness is so out of control and we're embarrassed at how we have succumbed.

I'm driving Maggie to school one day and innocently ask her which subject is her favorite. Maggie is silent. I look in the rearview mirror and see her sad eyes. She says, "Mom, can I not have a favorite? Please?" I get home and Google "China, adoption, mood, disorder."

After I had Maggie, when my pregnant friends would worry about whether they were going to go back to work after the baby, I'd tell them, "The first year it doesn't really matter who takes care of them. All they need is someone to give them a bottle, change their diaper, keep them warm." Of course, now I see that Sally is karmic payback for my smug attitude. Sally was fed, changed, and kept warm—and that's it. And the wounds run so deep that two years after we've gotten her Sally still doesn't like to be kissed on the face. She says it hurts.

REACTIVE ATTACHMENT DISORDER, RAD, IS what my Internet search turned up. After reading the list of symptoms—repetitive questions, controlling behavior, saying ouch when touched or kissed—I called Walter Buenning, Dr. B, the RAD guy, who said he'd come for the weekend. He lives in New Mexico and does intensive weekend sessions. Fourteen hundred dollars a day plus airfare, hotel, and per diem. Oh, and lunch. He likes to eat with the families. "Lunch is a great time to observe behavior," he'd said. "I'll just have what you guys normally have." I don't think so.

After lunch the first day—homemade chicken enchiladas, mixed green salad, and strawberries—Dr. B asked if we were ready for a holding session, the cornerstone of his therapy. He understands that holding therapy has gotten a bad rap but says, if done properly, it's quite safe. And he feels kids like Sally need it, won't recover without it. He says if we're uncomfortable with the term "holding therapy," we can call it a long hug.

In a nutshell: Sally's attachment cycle was broken when she was abandoned. We don't know when or for how long she was alone, but we do know that most babies in China are abandoned at a few days old and at night. So there is Sally, a few days old, hungry, wet, cold, in the dark, and no one answers her cries. Even after she was picked up and brought to the orphanage, there was a baby-to-nanny ratio of 9 to 1. Sal cries and no one comes. It's hardwired into her that she is basically on her own. Dr. B's thing is that we have to go back to the time her attachment cycle was broken and hardwire a different outcome to her cry. She has to learn that it's okay to be dependent. She's not on her own. She needs to experience what it feels like to not be in control, to give over control to parents who will answer her cries. And since we feel the opposite of in control, the therapeutic benefits of the long hug are as much for us as for Sal.

We prepare the couch in the den. Put down a towel in case, Dr. B says calmly, she sweats profusely or vomits. We tell Maggie she can play on the computer while we do the long hug. She seems fine, relieved we've called in a professional. We tell Sally about the long hug, and she seems excited. She lies down on the couch willingly. I lie next to her. Tony sits by my side, my support. Dr. B pulls a chair up by our heads. He's going to coach us through. Sally's back is to the couch. I wrap my arms around her, put her legs between mine. We're facing each other, noses touching. She can't move. She tries to squirm away. Dr. B tells me to tell Sally that Mommy's in control. Sally starts to panic, struggles to escape, begs for freedom. Within two minutes she is soaked in sweat and screaming. This is to be expected, says Dr. B, and Tony and I are just supposed to calmly reassure her that we love her and that we are in charge. We will know when it's best to stop the hug, she doesn't need to worry.

Sally starts to insult me. I'm ugly, my nose is crazy, she tells me over and over. She hates me. She begs, "Let me go, I'll be good." Dr. B tells me to kiss her face. I do. She tries to bite me, she spits at me. I thought I would feel funny doing this in front of Dr. B, a stranger to us until a few hours ago, but he fades away, it's just me, Sal, and Tony and Dr. B's calm voice reassuring us, reassuring Sal. Mama's in charge. Mama knows best.

Our first long hug went on for forty-five minutes. But it could have been forty-five days. Time stopped.

Finally, Sally stops fighting. She relaxes into my arms. Tells me, begs me, to kiss her face. When we finally release her she doesn't go anywhere, she stays where she is, happy, calm, stroking my face as I stroke hers. It occurs to me that what I said to Maggie in China is true. Sally is a survivor. But when I said it then I meant it like a personality trait, something she was born with, like her brown eyes. Two years later, I know more. About Sally's strength, and my own. I know about Tony's steadfastness. Maggie's resilience. Now I know that Sally wasn't born a fighter, it's something she became because otherwise she would have died. Survivor is a description no mother would want her child to have earned at one year old.

Sally and I lie together after the long hug. She looks right into my eyes and I meet her gaze. Neither of us looks away.

You're in charge, right, Mom?

Right, Sal. I'm in charge.

And right then I feel like it's true.

OLIVER'S PINK BICYCLE
James Braly

MY FATHER IS A DECORATED bomber pilot—World War II, Korea. Shot down, parachuted to safety. Along with all the men in his crew.

One time I asked him, "Dad? What was going on in the cockpit on the way down?"

He said, "All the men were blubberin' and cryin', 'I don't want to die, Captain Braly! I don't want to die!'"

I said, "I can understand that, Dad. What were you doing?"

He said, "Solvin' the problem. Cryin' doesn't solve a goddamn thing."

My dad's a man's man. Not a lot of room for weakness or fear. Not a lot of tolerance for differences.

One time I asked him to come see me playing in my high

school rock band. I was going through my English Glam Rocker phase: I had Farrah hair, and a shiny red jacket cinched at the waist and open to the navel, to frame my sunken English Rocker chest.

At the end of the gig he walked over, and I said, "Dad, what'd you think?"

He said, "You don't have a shirt on, boy."

So after twenty-five years of psychotherapy, inpatient and out, I decided that if and when the time came, I was going to be a very different kind of father—the kind who accepted the differences in his kids.

Now I'm a dad. I have two boys—Owen, who's eight months old, and Oliver, who's three and a half.

And Oliver's favorite color is pink. Not my favorite color, but I'm okay with that. I'm a father who accepts differences in his sons.

It started with pink crayons and moved on to the pink open-toed sandals. Continued with my wife's pink nail polish, which I actually started to think was kind of cute on the tips of Oliver's little fingers. I was even okay with the pink barrette, which Oliver kept in his pink purse for safekeeping when he wasn't wearing it.

Then one day, the summer before he turned three, Oliver came to me and said, "Daddy, for my birthday, can I have a pink bike?"

Even for me, this was a little too much pink, a bike being a permanent and public display of what it means to be a boy . . . and that boy's dad.

So I said, "Maybe." Thinking, *Maybe not.* To give myself a little time to mull it over.

The more I thought about it, the more it seemed to me that

the real issue wasn't that pink is for girls and therefore Oliver shouldn't have a pink bike. The issue was that he should have a red bike. *Just like I'd had.*

So I spent the next three months trying to make him come around to my point of view, using a technique that I'd learned from my mother: to make my thoughts seem like his. In the case of Oliver, that meant wandering around the neighborhood together and noticing the shiny red objects, especially the fire engines, and remarking, "Now *that* would be a great color for a bike, Oliver. Don't you think?"

To which Oliver would respond, "I want a fire engine! *And* a pink bike!!"

After three months of this, I finally accepted that I had failed at converting Oliver. That, in fact, he and I were different human beings, and that for his birthday I was going to buy him a pink bike.

Which is not easy. You can get a Barbie 2000 bike in pink. And you can get a Hello Kitty bike in pink. And Little Miss Puddin' and Jazz and the Charmer, all in pink. But you cannot get a plain pink bike, without some looking, and in some cases, encountering resistance from the marketplace.

I went to one shop run by a Jamaican fellow. When he saw Oliver and me walk in holding hands, and I told him what we wanted, he said, "Oh, no. Don't do dat ta heem, maan. Day keel heem on the playground." I said, "What would you recommend?" He led us to the boys' section of the shop and showed us the Turn 'n' Burn, the Thruster, the Piranha, and the Convict Junior, which featured a bike-sized decal of a wild-eyed escaped jailbird with broken handcuffs dangling from his wrists—in black or midnight blue.

I visited the Web site of every bike manufacturer in North

America, every big box retailer, and called or visited every bike shop in Manhattan, from Canal to 125th Street, before I finally found what I was looking for in the back room of a little place near the Hudson River: no name, no decals, pink.

On the morning Oliver turned three, it was sitting on the sidewalk outside his nursery school, wrapped in a pink crepe bow, me kneeling behind it.

The nursery school was next door to Mayor Bloomberg's mansion, so the street was filled with policemen. One walked over and said, "Daughter's birthday, huh?" And he smiled. I looked up and said, "Actually . . . it's my son's." The smile went away, and so did the policeman.

The door to the school opened. Oliver stepped out holding my wife's hand and saw the bike, me kneeling on the sidewalk behind it, and he started walking at an angle, stunned by the sight, taking it all in with a smile on his face before running straight for the handlebars and stopping at the last minute and looking down at me, saying, "Daddy, whose bike is this?"

"It's yours, Oliver. Happy birthday."

A few minutes later, I found myself trotting behind him through Central Park. The paths were filled with lines of little kids holding rings-on-strings tied to their teachers, leading them back to class after recess. As Oliver rode past them, they pointed at him with their free hands, boys and girls. Just like the Jamaican guy had warned. I wanted to snap their little fingers off. It felt like they were pointing at me.

Oliver didn't notice. He just kept riding, through the park, back to our building, into the playroom. Which we had decorated for the occasion in pink: streamers hanging from the chandelier; balloons; birthday cake, candles; and, after he parked it in the corner, Oliver's pink bike.

One by one his friends started to arrive and park their bikes next to Oliver's, including his best friend, Jeremy, who rode the Mountain Cub. In dark boy blue. With yellow paw-print decals.

Jeremy looked at Oliver's bike. Back at his. Back at Oliver's. Then he ran over to his mom and started crying.

"Mommy! I want a pink bike! Just like Oliver!"

Part of me felt this malevolent glee: sticking it to the tough kid with the pink shiv.

But another part of me thought, *You know what, Jeremy? So do I. Why does Oliver get a pink bike? We should get one, too. Everyone should get one!*

That's when I saw the gift that Oliver had given me for his birthday: the beauty and the power of being yourself. And of letting others be themselves.

It's not an easy gift to accept. A few weeks later, Oliver asked for a pink play dress, which is currently hanging up in his pink closet.

YAHOOEY!

Christie Mellor

A FEW YEARS AGO, YAHOO hired me to write a column for a big Lifestyle page they were launching. A fun, irreverent bit of parenting humor and advice that I would post a few times a week. I'd even be allowed to use excerpts from my book, *The Three-Martini Playdate*. It would be a delightful little bite of something that Yahoo readers could gulp down with their morning coffee: At least, that's how the nice Yahoo lady described it. I would be on the same page with Julia Sweeney and Oprah. Me and Oprah and Julia, just hanging out, talking parenting and relationships and stuff.

The launch was postponed, so Yahoo had the bright idea to temporarily house my column on the Yahoo Health page. In the Experts section, where doctors, psychologists, and other "expert" bloggers hold forth on various health-related topics. My column, so adorably titled "Gin & Colic" by my husband, would now share a page with Fitness, Diet, Diabetes, and Sex Advice.

I sent off a handful of "Gin & Colic" columns to the nice Yahoo people. A few weeks later, I checked in to see how the column looked, all fresh and shiny and expert. True, it wasn't me and Julia and Oprah yet, but it was still really cool to be thought of as an expert of any kind by anybody. Even though I'm always saying, "Oh, I'm not an expert, I'm just a mom with a lot of opinions," I secretly really do think I'm an expert, because my opinions about stuff are really good, and I like to spout my mouth off about them. Plus, I thought the Yahoo Health page could use a little humor. I mean, Diet and Fitness, sheesh. Eat some vegetables, walk around the block, and then relax with a cocktail, for God's sake.

So I clicked to the Yahoo Health page, ready to bask in the glow of my biting yet gentle humor. Yahoo had posted four or five of my columns, the latest being a reworking of a Helpful Hint from my book. I recommend that parents can get their kids to eat by inviting a young couple, or a bachelor, over for dinner. Preferably a southern bachelor, because southern bachelors are unfailingly polite and will go into raptures over your cooking. Especially after they've polished off half your bourbon. I merely propose that such colorful role models are good for children; that kids are more likely to eat what's in front of them if they witness a charming gentleman effusively praising their mom's cooking and asking for seconds. Soon, I suggest, your children will be wolfing down heaps of, say, braised kale with lemon and olives.

I sipped my coffee and read my amusing little column, just

like the Yahoo lady said Yahoo readers would be doing. There seemed to be an enormous number of comments. Cool! I scrolled down to the Comments section.

The first one kinda jumped out at me, what with the hate-filled invective and the name-calling. "This nut case has got to go," said RUStorm12. "If you think this is bad, try going back and reading some of her other drunken advice on child-rearing. This woman shouldn't be allowed within miles of children."

RUStorm12 continued, "She gives the worst parenting advice I have ever heard—if she is a parent, I feel *REALLY* sorry for that child. She's borderline on Social Services needing to intervene." She added: "Anyone who writes a book called *The Three-Martini Playdate* has no business being a mother, much less giving advice to others."

Another dissatisfied reader wrote, "Who the hell gave her this blog site? YOU (Ms. Mellor) are a drunk-whore! BTW: What the hell is Braised Kale with lemon and olives??"

I was mortified. But honestly, who would read my stuff and seriously think I'm giving *exact instructions* on how to raise a child? How could these people have missed the point so entirely?

Unless I really am a drunk who has no business raising kids. I mean, that's the secret fear of most parents, isn't it? Not the drunk part, necessarily, but that we have no idea what we're doing? And here I am writing books telling people what kind of parents I think they should be. Which adds a whole other dimension of insecurity, like what if I'm not only a bossy know-it-all, what if I'm a bossy know-it-all who's totally screwing up my kids? We're all going to screw up our kids a little—but what if I am truly wrong? Because when you fuck up with a cocktail in your hand, it just . . . looks bad.

Okay, I think parents are too overprotective, so I let my kids ride their bikes around sketchy Los Angeles neighborhoods. Well, actually, it's *our* neighborhood, but still! Other parents think it's sketchy and seem shocked that our kids ride their bikes around it. I let my kids take the public bus *in Los Angeles*, a place where normal, good parents spend their days driving kids to activities and playdates. And I don't have Family Night! Well, I guess we do, but we don't *call* it Family Night! We should start calling it Family Night! Also, I really *do* have a southern bachelor who loves my cooking and my bourbon—you think I make this shit up?

And . . . I feed my kids braised kale. With lemon and olives. And they eat it.

The braised kale reference inspired heated debate. RU-Stormi2 sniffed that I was "not a true wife and mother. I live in the south and can't imagine one man I know eating that—now, properly fried chicken, mashed potatoes, corn on the cob, and just to make sure he's happy some biscuits and milk gravy . . . "

I was starting to get a little miffed. Shame was giving way to annoyance. It's one thing to be called a drunken whore, but now they were insulting my cooking.

Then someone named Angel114 introduced a more sinister angle, chiming in with "I would be very leery of leaving my children with a single man who has no children of his own, especially in this day and age with all these sexual predators around. What kind of advice is this?"

Okay, I was merely acknowledging how difficult it can be to get finicky youngsters to eat a variety of different foods, and saying that an adult who is not a parent can often help them to expand their culinary repertoire. Apparently some readers took this to mean "leave your child alone with a pedophile." One reader submitted that I was really inviting "male prostitutes" over and trading my "services" for theirs.

RUStormi2 enlisted her friends to write in. One commented—and I reproduce it exactly:

> You are a very good example of what this world does not need
> for a parent, hire a bachelor that would be like the man going
> out on the street corner hiring a hooker to come to dinner.
> YAHOO, have you gone completely bananas, having this per-
> son giving advice.

The mudslinging was becoming a bit . . . excessive. I mean, what if I *do* think that children are not always wonderful and sweet and that they have terrible manners? What if I do think parents should have a grown-up life that is not entirely centered around their children? What if I do admit—maybe after a few drinks—that I enjoy a cocktail? Did that really mean I was a bitch who deserved a good raping, as one reader suggested?

I posted a response, stirring up a whole new batch of comments. Several people came out of the woodwork to defend me. Well-meaning readers opined that my columns were possibly being misinterpreted. RUStormi2 railed against the insurgents. Infighting broke out. The Comments section took on a life of its own.

Then the Yahoo people asked me to come in for a meeting.

They were so sorry. They'd really made a mistake putting me on the Health Experts page. It would be best, they said, to pull the column now. Wait until the Lifestyle page was launched. "But," I said, "won't it seem like the crazy people have won?"

Yes, it would, and it did. However, caving in to the crazy but vocal minority was apparently the most cost-effective way out for the corporate minds at Yahoo.

But what a learning experience. First of all, I found out it's really important to know your audience. This was not my audience. I was hated by a mob of people because I eat braised kale with lemon and olives. I was hated for drinking martinis and for being flippant about alcohol. I was possibly suspected of having liberal sympathies and liking French cheese. If I were a true wife and mother, I would be home making fried chicken with milk gravy. Milk gravy! I don't even know what milk gravy is!

For many months, I couldn't get milk gravy out of my mind. "If only I made milk gravy!" I would think. "Our car would never have broken down!" Or, "If only I made milk gravy!" Shaking my tiny fist at the heavens. "I would still be writing for Yahoo with Oprah and Julia!"

THE BUGABOO

Andrew McCarthy

MY PARTNER LOVES HER BUGABOO. I've hated it since the day we got it. It's easy to hate. After you buy the rain cover and the car seat attachment and the mosquito net and the Breezy Sun Canopy and the parasol and the Snuggly Foot Muff and the latte cup holder and the grocery bag hook and the custom diaper bag and the Transport Bag, it tops out at well over a thousand dollars. A thousand dollars for a stroller. My first car cost me less than that. For a thousand dollars you can feed a family of five in Sri Lanka for a year. And try to get the fucking thing into the trunk of a taxi while cars pile up behind you on a busy street.

There is one day I remember in particular; I was trying to break down our Bugaboo and put it on the bus after a day by the sea in Dunleary, Ireland (don't ask me about getting it on a plane) because the bus driver would not allow it on board except in the folded condition and was threatening to leave me by the roadside as I struggled to collapse the metal frame. As I waged war on the base of my partner's beloved Bugaboo, she watched through the window—as did the entire bus—with our precious daughter clutched to her breast, while my son from my previous marriage pressed his nose against the glass, steaming the window. Finally Dolores sent out Sam, age five, to help.

"Daddy, you just press the hooks down and back, not up. No, Daddy, no, no, don't jam it."

"Sam," I said to my son, as I unclenched my teeth, "Daddy knows how to do it." Memories of my explosive father and his overheated Jaguar in the middle of Harlem in 1973 on the way to Yankee Stadium with my eleven-year-old self and my best friend David Autry crammed into the jump seat in back suddenly leaped into my mind. After my father's display of misplaced anger that afternoon, David never came to my house again. "Just get back on the bus, sweetheart, Daddy will be right there," I told Sam, conscious of my feelings of superiority to my father even in this moment of near physical violence.

"No, you won't, Daddy. You don't know how to do it."

"Sam, please, just get back on the bus; I will get a taxi and meet you and Dolores and Willow back in Dublin," I said—and secretly decided I would throw the Bugaboo into the North Sea, just a few yards away, after the bus had departed.

"No, Daddy, here, look, I'll show you." My son reached for the culprit, a small silver handle that would not respond to my insistent jabbing.

"Sam. Please," I said, my voice rising, my frustration mounting, "just . . . get . . . on—" At that moment God asserted himself into my life and the cross bar released and the wheels folded over and the Bugaboo base collapsed and I hoisted the now properly folded contraption up and onto the bus as passengers leaned far back in their seats, eyes averted, while I stormed down the aisle, fury masking my humiliation. For the duration of the forty-minute ride back to Dublin, I sat on the upper level of the bus, fuming, far away from my family, who sat on the main level below me. Naturally, I blamed my partner for all this. Not only had she wasted one thousand dollars of our money, but also she had clearly ruined my life.

As the bus lurched back toward Dublin, the thought settled in on me—albeit six years late—that my life had really and truly changed beyond any recognition of its former incarnation.

I took stock.

I was divorced—*I'm not the kind of guy who gets divorced*, I told myself. I have two small children by two different women—*What do I, play in the NBA?* I scolded myself. And I divide my time poorly between New York and Ireland, living in neither place peacefully, having succeeded only in doubling my budget and belonging to the worst frequent flyer program in the sky. *How did this happen to me, how?* I demanded as the bus lumbered through a kind of suburban hell.

The facts were easy to trace. I had married my college sweetheart (after twenty years of thinking it over), we then had a child, who was the culmination of our youthful love, and we split. I met a woman and after four days she moved to America; a week later, she was pregnant. That all seemed kind of quick, except for some of the days early on when the morning sickness was in full bloom, those days seemed long—very long. It was then, during protracted solitary afternoon walks in the woods, that I decided I would move to Bolivia, alone. But then our daughter was born and love saved the day. So that's how I got to be on the bus in Ireland, that much was clear—but like I said, those are just facts. So much of the *why* of it all has remained a mystery to me.

But as the bus inched along, stopping to take on ever more suburbanites escaping their torpor for a night in the big city, I told myself, *Hey, it's normal that I'm just now realizing how different my life is, a lot has happened, fast, and I'm just getting my head above water. Maybe it's because I'm on the second tier of the bus that I can suddenly see so clearly*, I concluded, and patted myself on the back for retaining such a good sense of humor in difficult times. But whatever the reason, the veil was dropping, and it was becoming clear to me what perhaps should have been clear from the very start: My simple, well-ordered life would never come back again. And to make matters worse, the realization dawned on me that I was no longer calling all the shots, and the few I was calling went challenged, disregarded, or unheard; the one or two that were acquiesced to proved even more disastrous—clearly I could not run all our lives.

Running my own life when I was alone, it was easy to fool myself into thinking that I was doing a terrific job orchestrating things. After all, there was no one around to contradict me, and, hey, maybe I was, goddamn it, but with a new partner I was still getting to know—I wasn't even sure if she liked me yet—I was making one wrong move after the next. And as we disembarked from the bus and crammed into her parents' car, I felt like the teenager I had not been in many, many years. I tried to laugh along as my struggles with the Bugaboo were recounted in the car and again later that evening at the family dinner table. But I felt alone in it all, isolated and misunderstood. Then, as everyone around me heartily dove into a dessert I proudly refused out of self-pity, and I watched my son attack gob after gob of chocolate ice cream, a good portion of it actually finding its way into his mouth, and I looked on as my daughter pinched and plucked raisins from the tabletop and proudly gummed them into submission, and as I saw my partner chatting so effortlessly with her family (something I could never do), I felt suddenly like the Grinch who stole Christmas, when he's atop Mt. Crumpit: My heart seemed to verily burst open and all the love I normally hold in check, for fear of being decimated by its loss or by its rejection, poured out. I sat motionless as a feeling of calm and well-being descended upon me, a feeling that I would not admit to anyone until much, much later—once it had safely receded. But there was no denying that it has left its mark, like a high tide line in the sand on the morning after a full moon.

It's easy to misassign to your loved one emotions that belong to yourself; after all, that's what relationships are for—deflecting responsibility. But it takes a certain maturity to deflect things onto inanimate objects. And the Bugaboo has proven to be a perfect receptacle for my occasional fits of resentment at my situation—a situation which amounts to my loving more than I ever thought I could, and certainly more than I would like, and allowing myself to be loved by more people than I ever thought I would. And in that love I have come to realize just how little say I have and just how lucky I am to be so far out on an emotional limb. God bless the fucking Bugaboo.

THE FAMILY BED

Rick Cleveland

PARENTHOOD, LIKE POLITICS, IS A completely partisan endeavor. George Lakoff, the linguistics professor who wrote *Moral Politics*, says that Republicans are like paternalistic, tough-love, corporal-punishment-doling dads who think their kids should act responsibly and pull themselves up by their own bootstraps and never ever ask anyone for a handout, and that Democrats on the other hand are like compassionate, gentle, earth-mothering moms who would never spank their offspring, and in fact believe their kids should live at home until they're thirty—or, seeing as how forty is the new thirty, until they're forty—and that they should have all their meals cooked for them, their laundry done for them, their every need met and whim nurtured.

So as a parent, you're either a Republican or a Democrat.

To further subdivide us, you're either a Ferberizer or a Searsist.

Dr. Richard Ferber, the director of the Center for Pediatric Sleep Disorders at Children's Hospital in Boston, is famous for the "let them cry it out" method of "sleep training." This is the method that most of our parents used, and that most Americans have used for generations, and sadly (to my view) still use.

It involves simply putting your infant child in his or her crib in a room down the hall at a designated time every evening, closing the door, and then leaving him or her in there—pretty much no matter what—so that he or she will learn to "self-soothe," at first by crying him or herself to sleep. This, in my opinion, is the Republican way of trying to get your kids to sleep through the night. It emphasizes the primacy of the parents' lives over that of their child. I also believe it's a vestigial piece of philosophy left over from previous generations who believed that children should be seen but not heard. Because, in fact, they are very much heard. They are heard screaming from behind closed doors as they are being "trained."

Like Dr. Ferber, Dr. William Sears was trained at Harvard's Children's Hospital in Boston. He is a pediatrician and a father of eight children (which I find totally unnecessary), and he is most famous for the philosophy behind "attachment parenting." The school of attachment parenting is big on breastfeeding and is pretty much the antithesis of Ferberization. It is also responsible for the promotion of the "family bed."

The family bed is that hippie-ish, giant, futon-like mass covered with pillows where everyone—Mom, Dad, infants, toddlers, older siblings, the family dog and cat, and possibly Mom or Dad's out-of-work younger brother or the nanny—goes to not get a good night's sleep. In many people's minds it's a slightly skeevy place that fosters molestation.

Between the two of them, Ferber and Sears have written dozens of books on the care and feeding of infants and small children. When I was an infant there was pretty much only one book on the subject: *Dr. Spock's Baby and Child Care.*

Breast-feeding was actually controversial back in those days—Dr. Spock thought that breast milk wasn't nutritious enough—and it was also socially unacceptable. Despite this, my mom breast-fed me. While she smoked. Dr. Spock didn't say anything about not smoking while breast-feeding, and crazily enough, he also didn't say anything about not smoking while being pregnant.

I don't really know if my mom smoked while she nursed me, but she was a multitasker, and she did a lot of things while smoking, so it's a fair assumption that she smoked while I nursed. I think she nursed me for about a month, then switched me over to formula. How I handled the nicotine withdrawal I don't remember.

When my wife and I started dating, she was a single parent and worked full-time.

Because they didn't see each other all day during the week, sleeping in the same bed became a crucial part of creating and sustaining the mother-and-child bond.

So when Mary and I started dating, I slept out in the living room, on the sofa. I slept on that sofa for months.

After we moved in together, all three of us slept in the same bed, with our daughter Clara in the middle.

After our twin sons, Gus and Charlie, were born, we got a bigger bed. Actually we got two beds. One was a California king, and the other was an extralong twin. We jammed them together and created our version of the family bed. It took up approximately three-quarters of the floor space in our bedroom.

I slept on one side of the California king, Gus slept next to me, Mary slept next to him, Charlie slept in the crack between the two beds, and Clara slept in the extralong twin.

We lived in Topanga Canyon, where lots of people raise their children in family beds—perhaps out of fear of coyotes or mountain lions. But in the city, my coworkers and friends would often ask me what it was like, this "sleeping-with-your-wife-and-kids-in-the-same-bed business."

They wondered whether I was afraid of smothering or squishing them.

They also wondered at what age the family bed ended. Didn't children who were reared in a family bed become creepily attached to their parents? What about when they became teenagers? What if they still wanted to sleep with you then? And what about you and your wife's sex life? Did you guys even have one?

When friends drove all the way out to our house, they would often ask to see our family bed. They wanted to know what on earth it looked like. Even though the family bed lived in our "bedroom," some friends marveled at how much floor space we had devoted to the actual practice of "sleeping."

Most of our friends from the city could not get their heads wrapped around the idea of parents sleeping with their children. Even though it's the norm in more cultures than it isn't, in North America, it is seen as far too communal. After all, didn't the Mansons sleep in a family bed?

Meanwhile, many of those same friends were having babies

and putting them in cribs in bedrooms down the hall far from their own bedrooms and enduring long nights of letting their babies "cry it out." The more resolve you show, the stronger your babies will become when they grow older.

One friend of mine who was Ferberizing his son told me that it was working beautifully—until his son got old enough to figure out how to climb out of his crib. My friend then put a kind of lid on the top of the crib with a latch on it, and when he showed it to me, I thought, *What's the difference between this crib and a cage?*

Now, to be fair, if I had fallen in love with a woman who had Ferberized her daughter, I would have probably been okay with Ferberizing our sons.

And to be honest, when my friends from work asked me a lot of questions about our family bed, I would start to wonder if maybe someday one of my kids might go into therapy because of it, or even worse, write a book or a one-person show about it.

In the end, I got totally behind it when my wife put it to me like this: "Bears don't make their cubs sleep in caves down the hill from their caves." And that's so true. If a mother bear let her offspring "cry it out," surely they would be eaten by wolves or mountain lions.

And even though it's true that we aren't bears, we are mammals—we nurse our young, and we should, I think, keep them close, especially in those first few years, because I believe that keeping them close will make them stronger, more independent, and less afraid of the world.

Some of you Ferberizers out there might disagree. And if you want to hold on to the primacy of your adulthood and act like a Republican—well, it's a free country. But I say, surrender to the family bed. It's a hell of a lot cozier.

My daughter is eleven now, my sons are almost nine, and all three of them have moved into their own bedrooms. Now, most nights, it's just me, my wife, Keith Olbermann, and one of our three cats. I have to say, I like having the extra leg room. On some nights, though, it feels like there's way too much room in there.

WHAT GROWN-UPS DO

Brett Paesel

THE UPSIDE OF GETTING OLDER is that you hardly give a fuck anymore. The word "hardly" is important here. Because just when you're sure you've abandoned all feeling about what people think about you or say about you or promise-and-don't-deliver to you, a teenage grocery store checker says you look tired on a Saturday morning and you burst into tears, drop the bottle of vodka you were buying for Bloody Marys, and run out to the parking lot, choking on snot and obscenities until your husband pulls the car around to load you in like a wounded dog. We've all had little moments like this. Still, for the most part, as we get older, we give a fuck of a lot less than we did before. Which is one of the few beauties of aging.

By the time I had my first son at thirty-nine and my second

at forty-three, I was sure that I was finally mature enough to raise children. Gone was the impetuous, highly emotional, impoverished, self-righteous young woman I'd been through my twenties and early thirties. Gone was the woman who thought it was a good idea to stay up all night doing cocaine before a 4:00 A.M. flight to London, rather than getting some sleep. Taking her place was a wiser woman. One who was calmer, more generous, less rash. One who was capable of thinking through problems and weighing options, rather than exploding in unfocused and futile rage, the way I did the night my boyfriend told me that he would *have* to sleep with Isabella Rossellini if the opportunity ever presented itself. True, I wasn't as young and pretty as the other mommies, but, I assured myself, I would be well served by my years, able to guide my children with Buddha-like serenity and insightful good humor.

SPENCER'S MIND IS NOT ON his homework. This isn't surprising for a second-grade boy, and it's the reason that I sit next to him, a reluctant taskmaster. His distraction tonight has a different quality, however. This time it's not a football game or a joke he's heard or his birthday party that preoccupies him.

"One more page," I coax.

He sighs; looks down at his math paper.

"What is it?"

"Nothing."

"You can tell me."

A pause and then, "Well. Um."

He struggles for words, tenses his face, fingers the paper.

"It's okay," I say, "take your time."

It's clear that there's something he wants to tell me. It's also clear that he's conflicted. Is he worried about how I will react? Quite possibly. This is where my experience and maturity come into play. Instead of bursting into tears and begging him to tell Mommy everything so she doesn't worry herself into an irreversible coma, I let my face go slack. I flatten my voice. I become the embodiment of reason and good judgment. "I won't be mad at you, Spencer," I say. "You can tell me anything. We'll work it out."

"Today on the bus ... " He tears the corner of the paper.

"Yes," I say calmly.

"On the bus ... "

"On the bus."

"On the bus. Martin took my jacket."

"You brought your jacket home."

"Yeah. But Martin took it and threw it around the bus."

"Oh," I say blankly.

"I had to chase it."

"But you got it back."

"Sam got it for me. Then ... " He starts to tear his paper again. "Martin took my outer space book and threw it around so I had to chase it."

"Did you get it back?"

"Yeah. But that time even Sam threw it around. The whole bus ... " He closes his eyes and scrunches his face. "The whole bus threw my book around and made me chase it."

"Oh, honey." I reach over and put my hand over his forearm while he continues to fiddle with the paper. "Who's Martin?" *Little shit, whoever he is. I'll break him. I'll walk over to his house right now and call him out and kick him. Kick him? I can't kick him. He's a child. I'm not a monster. I'll yell at him, that's what I'll do. I'll scream at him on his own front lawn so all the neighbors know what a weasly little shit he is. Okay. Okay. Wait. Slow down. Slow down. Get the story. Get the facts.*

Spencer looks out the window. "Martin is a fifth grader."

A fifth grader!!! Picking on my little second grader? What the fuck? What kind of lawless jungle is that bus? I'll yank that little fucker Martin off the bus. I'll haul his ass out onto the sidewalk and . . . and . . . and I'll scream at him. I'll take one of his books and throw it around to the adults. Show him what it's like. We'll see how he likes feeling helpless and humiliated.

Practicing stillness, projecting calm, I ask, "Has Martin done stuff like this before?"

"Martin and James rule the bus."

"Rule the bus?"

"They took Amanda's headband and spit on it."

"Both Martin and James?"

"James only does it because Martin does it."

"Spits on headbands and throws books around?"

"Yeah."

I breathe in. Everything slows down. My thoughts stop racing and narrow into a pinprick of consciousness centered in my forehead. Deliberate calm infuses my body. I feel steely, methodical, dangerous. Like the Terminator.

"Did you tell Martin to stop it?"

"Sure I did."

"And he kept torturing . . . Sorry. He kept throwing your book around?"

"I told you."

"Well, Spencer. The first thing you need to know is that you are a great kid who doesn't deserve to be treated this way."

"I know," he says with a shrug that indicates a bit of waffling on this fine point.

"You're a great kid, Spencer. And Martin is a bully. Bullies are all about power. They want to upset you. They want to see you cry. So the first thing to do is act like you don't care. If you don't react, it won't be any fun for Martin and he'll stop doing it."

Spence shrugs again.

"Did you cry?"

"No."

"Good. I know I say that it's okay to cry. And it is. But if you can manage it, try not to cry in front of a bully."

A tear slides down Spence's face.

"You can cry now. With me. It's okay."

"Okay . . . " Another tear.

"Come here," I say. Spence scoots out of his chair and climbs into my lap, tucking his lanky legs under him so he's a ball. He makes himself small and babylike in my lap, and I curl myself over his rounded back, cooing and humming into his hair while he cries.

When his crying subsides, he raises himself up, leans against my chest, unfolds his legs, and lets them hang loose. We sit like this for a while. I look out the window at the dark night, feeling the damp weight of my boy.

After a few minutes, I shift. "So we have a plan. You're going to work on ignoring bullies. And I promise to make sure that Martin never bothers you again."

MY HUSBAND, PAT, HAS BEEN playing poker all evening. He comes home and slips into bed while I'm on the computer. By the time I climb in bed he's sleeping solidly, so I don't have a chance to talk to him about the bully. I look up at the ceiling and wait for sleep. After five minutes I throw the covers off, sit up, lie back down, pull the covers back over me, switch sides, fluff the pillow, pull another pillow close, get up, turn on the light, look at the titles of the books on my shelves, lie back down, turn off the light, throw aside the covers. All while I consider various plans of how to make good on my promise about Martin to Spence. I think about waking Pat to run the plans by him, but waking Pat in the middle of the night should only be done in the event of an earthquake or fire. It takes two minutes of repeated pounding on his back to rouse him, at which point he bolts up and looks around furiously, yelling, "What? What? What?" before falling back onto his pillow in a dead sleep. The whole process has to be repeated at least two more times before he will stay awake and focus on my mouth moving. After I stop talking, he will mumble, "I don't care," and pass out again.

It's clear to me that the best way to stop Martin from bullying Spence is to scare the living shit out of him. I could probably get Pat to do this. He's tall and has a deep voice. But he might be *too* scary. In which case, Martin could call the school or tell his parents. I want to avoid landing on the local news as the interfering, obsessed parents just one step shy of the Texas mom who solicited a hit man to kill her daughter's rival. No, to avoid that, I should do it—preferably without eyewitnesses. That way, if Martin rats me out it'll be my word against a fifth grader's. I'm pretty sure the principal will come down squarely on my side. She looks like kids stopped being fun for her twenty years ago.

It feels like hours before my body gets heavy on the mattress. I don't want to dream about the sandbox, but I do. Is it a dream? My sleep is light, if it's sleep at all. I feel awake or on the edge of consciousness all night. Whatever my state, I am submerged enough in memory and altered reality to find myself sitting on the edge of a sandbox on the playground of a military housing area. It's 1963. Several other children sit on the edge of the sandbox alternately scowling at me and watching my parents rake the sand. One of the bits of reality I've altered is the fact that I can see the children's faces. If this were real, I wouldn't be able to see faces because what my parents are looking for with that rake is my glasses. I lose them in the sandbox once every week or so. This time the glasses are lost because Jimmy Oliensis hid them when I took them off to rub my eyes. Jimmy sits with the rest of the children, looking impassive, like the sociopath I'm sure he matured into.

Nothing much happens in the dream, and I've had it before. Me on the edge, staring at Jimmy, who stares back, unblinking. Me enduring the other kids' annoyance and derision because their play has been interrupted. My parents painstakingly raking from one side of the sandbox to the other, eventually unearthing the glasses. My father dusting them off and placing them back on my face.

"Everyone back in the sand," my mother says.

The kids crowd the sandbox, and I feel . . .

What? What do I feel?

The dream stops here.

I am awake. My thoughts flip over to Spence. I'm not a child anymore. He's the child. He's my child. How did I get a child?

I shove a pillow off the bed and turn onto my side. I open my eyes, grab my glasses, and look at the clock. Two more hours until the alarm. I take off my glasses, put them back on the nightstand, roll onto my back, and stare at the ceiling again.

———

I OPEN MY EYES AND look at the clock, minutes before the alarm, and turn it off. Padding into the bathroom with stealth, I turn on the shower and get in. I feel like a soldier preparing for battle. I lean my head back into the stream, clearing my mind of clutter, concentrating only on the task at hand.

Spence is already up reading when I walk into the living room.

"Morning, sweetheart," I say innocently.

"Hi, Mom."

I slip into the kitchen to get Spencer's breakfast ready. *Good,* I think. *His "Hi, Mom" sounded light, naive. He is completely unaware of my dark intentions.*

On the walk to the bus, Spence hops around me, talking about basketball. At least I think it's basketball. It's some team he likes. I'm not listening, but I drop an occasional "Really?" or "Oh" to create the illusion of normalcy.

As we approach the bus stop, I see the gathered parents and children as if through a fish-eye lens. Spencer runs ahead of me and stands in line as I plant myself in my usual spot next to an Armenian dad with a daughter who keeps getting in trouble for standing up when the bus is moving.

"Which of the kids is Martin?" I ask the dad.

"Over there," he says, nodding in the direction of a perfectly ordinary boy in a purple football jersey. I don't know what I was expecting—a cloven hoof, perhaps—but Martin isn't it. Never mind. I cannot cloud my purpose with extraneous thought.

I walk over to Martin, who's poking the ground with a stick. I look around and take a guess that I'm out of earshot of most of the parents, especially if I use the voice I'm planning on using.

"Are you Martin?" I hiss.

He looks up at me and squints. "Yeah."

"Good," I continue, narrowing my eyes. "I want you to know that if you mess with Spencer one more time, I will make sure you get removed from the bus—"

"What?" says Martin, interrupting my rhythm.

"*Permanently*," I conclude with a menacing smile.

Martin brings a hand up to shade his eyes.

"I didn't do anything," he says.

I take a step closer, looming over him, my back to everyone else at the bus stop.

"I know what you did," I say, bringing my hand up and jabbing two fingers in his direction like a hex sign as I warn him, ominously, "I am watching you."

Martin's eyes round in cartoon horror. *Mission accomplished,* I think, turning back around to the group assembled, all of whom seem completely unaware of my dealings. I look over at Spence bouncing up and down, talking excitedly to another kid. I breathe in with satisfaction and think to myself, *It takes more than a cocky-ass fifth grader to throw me off my game, motherfucker.*

WHEN I TALK TO SPENCER that evening and discern that Martin did, indeed, lay off him on the bus, I'm surprised that I feel no sense of triumph. I've had the entire day to consider other, more rational courses of action I could have taken. I could have called the school or talked to Martin's parents, for example. Isn't that what grown-ups do? I could have spoken calmly to Martin and Spencer together. Wouldn't that have been a more enlightened approach?

Shit. Just when you think you don't give a fuck about anything anymore, your kid knocks you off balance with a simple tale of school bus bullying, and suddenly you're threatening ten-year-olds with a sense of frontier justice that makes you less like a soccer mom and more like Cool Hand Luke.

Later that night, I drift to sleep much more easily. No doubt because I am depleted from my mission and the worry and the self-doubt and the imperfect, fanatical, ecstatic, and possibly homicidal love I feel for my boy.

Rolling onto my side, I let myself think what I haven't allowed myself to think all day. Of course, the child I was protecting today wasn't Spencer, who might have been able to handle it all by himself. The child I was protecting was me.

THE SACRIFICE
Lew Schneider

SO MUCH OF THE PARENTING experience is sacrifice. From the moment your first child is born you begin to lose yourself: You eat on someone else's schedule, you sleep on someone else's schedule, you shower on someone else's schedule. It's like you're in jail but you love the warden. As your kids grow, you continually forgo your own immediate gratification in exchange for a future benefit or important lesson. As parents we must be willing to give up something precious to help our children learn to navigate a complex and often unforgiving world.

I'd taken my son, Marty, who was about three at the time, to do errands in Santa Monica. At this point he was in the early months of wearing big-boy underpants. I was pretty vigilant about taking him to the bathroom before leaving the house or getting in the car, and so as we were getting ready to leave a store, I said, "Marty, how about you go pee?" He said that he didn't have to. I told him that we weren't going to be home for a little while and he maybe should just try. He seemed pretty adamant about not having to go, and since he was always fairly compliant and usually did go under these circumstances, I thought, *Maybe he's at the point where he knows his own body.* We went back to the parking garage, and before taking the elevator up to the car I asked again, "Do you want to go here? They have a bathroom." Again, he claimed he didn't. *Okay, fine. He doesn't have to go.* I got him into his car seat and we started winding our way down the ramp.

I had gone about twelve feet, or enough to lose my parking space, when my angel said, "I have to pee." Stealing one of my wife Liz's favorite lines, I called out nervously, "Tell the pee to stay in." I heard him whisper, "Stay in, pee." I continued desperately, "We'll find a bathroom." Then I started to admonish him. "Sweetie," I said through gritted teeth, "I asked you if you had to go and now we aren't really in a good place to go and now you have to go and there really isn't a place to go now." I don't know exactly what response I wanted from him at that point. An apology for my inconvenience would have been very mature but a real long shot. He just whimpered, "I really have to go."

By then I had reached the street. Dreading the prospect of pulling a urine-soaked car seat cover off and doing the laundry and, worse still, rethreading the seat harness straps back through the whole thing (easily a forty-five-minute job for me), I pulled quickly into a Bank of America parking lot. Since it was Sunday, the bank was closed, so I parked quickly and jumped out to get Marty. "Tell the pee to stay in, tell the pee to stay in," I continued to chant.

Marty whispered, "Stay in, pee," in his most serious tone as I yanked him from the car. In an instant I had him standing on a low cement wall, and I pulled his shorts and big-boy underpants down and sighed happily. "Way to go, pal, go ahead." I felt so relieved at that moment, it was like I was peeing.

I know, by the way, that you can't just pee in public. I myself had been traumatized by a mother who believed that if you were little, it was just fine to pee outside in nature. We would be on an outing and I would have to go, and she would point to a bush or tree or patch of grass or the most nature-y feature of the landscape and say, "Go over there." I would sort of sneak off very self-consciously and look back to see her urging me on. "Go ahead, no one can see." I would then look over my shoulder at people who were looking at me and think, *I can see them.* I would even say as much, and my mom's answer was "Well, no one is interested." Later on, as I developed a real working relationship with my own penis, I came to understand that in a way, she was right. But anyway . . . in this case, I was desperate and I'd saved myself a lot of aggravation.

At just that moment a Santa Monica mounted police officer—in this case mounted on a bicycle—arrived. He debiked and very sternly informed me that this wasn't okay. I knew it wasn't. I really knew. I had done everything short of letting Marty pee in his pants to avoid the situation. I was helpless at this point. By now Marty was finished and I'd pulled up his pants. The cop was explaining that I, or we, had broken the law and that we would have to face the consequences. At this point I had to defend myself, and I did. At Marty's expense. Up to this point in his life I'd always tried to be there to comfort, console, or nurture, but faced with the awesome display of power, albeit in

Lycra bike shorts, that the state was bringing to bear upon me, I cracked.

I declared, "I told him, officer. I swear to God, I asked, 'Do you have to pee?' And he said no. Tell him you said that, Marty! When we were at Restoration Hardware, I said, 'Let's try to go pee.' And you wouldn't. He wouldn't, officer. Then again in the garage, where the whole place smells like pee, I asked again and he said no again. You did, Marty!" I yammered on about how I thought we could make it home, but the cop countered, "Yeah, well, he can't just pee on things." The cop seemed to be reaching for his citation book or maybe his gun as I kicked it into high gear and practically shouted, "That's right, officer! He can't. Tell him. Tell him what happens when you break the law!" I moved right next to the cop, and we faced Marty as a united front.

Marty looked up like Oliver Twist just before he asked for more gruel. The officer was paralyzed. He looked down at the lad and then at me as I shook my finger at Marty, who was surely going to learn a very valuable lesson. The cop drew a deep breath and stammered something about how he couldn't do this but that I should try not to let this happen again. Then he saddled up and rode off. I was still shaking a little as I led Marty back to the car. He seemed a little uneasy around me for a while after that.

Replaying the event over in my head, I often think about how I might have handled it another way. Should I have defended Marty? Should I have taken the heat? Should I have argued with the cop, or pleaded for leniency? Nope, I congratulated myself. I handled that one exactly right. Aligning myself with the cop was a stroke of genius. I beat a pretty stiff ticket and certainly avoided the hassle of appearing in court to plead my case. I may have saved our lives. I'm telling you, that cop seemed like he was itching to shoot someone. And you know what? Marty's fine. He re-toilet-trained himself. He's now sixteen, and at six foot one he towers over me. I read this to him, and he laughed hard at the memory. Then he got a little contemplative. I could tell by the way he looked at me that he got it: Sometimes sacrifices have to be made.

I YELLED

Mo Gaffney

I WAITED TILL I WAS somewhat elderly to have a child. It didn't feel like I was waiting. I didn't think, *I'm going to hold off having a kid till it's almost physically impossible.* It just never came up, really. I wasn't one of those girls who planned my wedding at ten years old or had names picked out for my future kids. I grew up at a time where women were saying, "We don't have to get married and have kids, we can do anything! We can keep our own names and be CEOs." That sounded pretty good to me—not the CEO part but the other parts. I decided if it came up I'd think about it, but if not, no biggie. My womb wasn't pulsing in anticipation or anything. Then, when I was thirty-nine, my baby-daddy said, "Let's try to have a kid, we're getting old, we're missing the window." And I said, "Okay." You see,

I was pretty sure I *had* missed the window, so what harm would it do to try? My eggs could finally meet some sperm, not that they'd get involved or anything, and I could look back and say, "Well, God knows I tried. Not meant to be. My dogs are my children," or something like that. Then, *surprise!* My vengeful, slutty eggs hooked up with the first (and I mean *first*) sperm that came along and I got pregnant days shy of the big 4-0. As surprised as I was, I was also excited. *I'll be a good mom. I'll only have the one, and, well, it would be nice to think about someone other than myself.*

It's turned out okay for the most part. I mean, I'm not, like, soccer mom perfect. I can't cook or sew, and I've never been a fan of cartoons, but I like my kid most of the time. I think "playdate" is embarrassing to even *say*, but he gets his share. He has bunk beds even though his room is the size of a Honda Civic. I took him to LegoLand in hundred-degree heat while at the same time having frickin' hot flashes. And yes, I let him have a Mohawk. A full-on, head shaved, six-inch strip of brick-hard, straight-up Johnny Rotten Mohawk at eight years old. When we finally shaved it off he looked like a convict, and I don't know which was worse, but you get the idea. I'm a pretty okay mom.

My biggest challenge has been patience. On my best day I'm not a patient person, and—I don't know if you're aware of this—kids *require* patience. They test your every last nerve, and it's very difficult to reason with them. Somehow I've remained pretty calm. Not perfect, but not horrible either. Here's the thing, though: The other night I yelled at my nine-year-old, Jack. I don't mean I screamed at him for hours on end while looking for my bottle of scotch or anything. I just yelled, *"Stop it!"*

I'd asked him to put up the seat in the bathroom, and then I heard *bang...bang...bang...bang...bang...*, the seat hitting the toilet over and over like some monotonous Morse code for "yell at me immediately." And that's when I yelled *"Stop it"* in a really yelly voice. I hardly ever yell at him. I'll speak loudish or serious or exasperated or use my "I mean it" voice or even be sarcastic, but out-and-out yelling at Jack is kind of rare. Before I had a kid, I yelled whenever I wanted. Mostly at fellow motorists and boyfriends. I didn't even think about it. Who even stopped to think if they deserved it? I'd feel the need to yell and I'd yell. End of story. But the first time I yelled at my kid he visibly quaked, and I thought, *Oh, okay, shouldn't yell, I'll work on that.* So I consciously try not to yell at him. And I mostly succeed. What led up to me yelling at Jack this time was me asking him, like fourteen times, to put on his pajamas, then asking him about twenty times to brush his teeth. Usually I only have to ask three times for each, and I can deal with that, but this was one of those nights when he went temporarily deaf. Then I said, "Make sure you go potty, and remember to put the seat up, please." Then, well, the *bang bang bang* and the yell. I was possessed. I felt the yell boil up from my feet and *blammo*, it exploded out of me and shook the house. They probably heard my *"Stop it"* in France. My face was red and my hair stood up on my head. I turned around to see who that was that yelled so loud. Oh, it was me! It surprised my son when I yelled, but he wasn't intimidated by my yelling. He didn't immediately hop to or anything. He just got mad at me and yelled back. "I was trying to put it up!" he bellowed in a volume to match my own.

I think it was on *Oprah* where I heard some child expert say, "When you fight in front of your children you change who they are." I'm pretty sure, according to this theory, yelling at them would have the same effect. Prior to my yelling *"Stop it"* my son was no doubt going to become, I don't know, the poet laureate of the United States or the next Bono or something, and my yelling 86'd that. Some neuron in his brain fired, and now he'll torture ants and want to live in my garage till he's forty.

I'm sure there might be parents out there who never fight in front of their kids, or yell at them. The Amish or polygamous sects or anyone with seriously out-of-date clothing. (Or if they *are* up to date they have got to be on buckets of Valium or have three nannies or live in a separate wing or something.) But I consider myself a fairly decent parent and I yelled at my kid. This business of changing who they are seems a bit of a nebulous assertion. So you have one bad day, have a pissy little fight with your husband or wife or yell *"Stop it,"* and suddenly you've changed in some fundamental way who your child is? Wow. The question that plagues me now is, can you change them back? With, I don't know, therapy? Medication? Guitar Hero 3? I'm gonna go ahead and guess most people up to now *have* been changed, then. We would all probably be dressed in flowy white clothes with doves on our heads helping baby seals if our parents just hadn't yelled. But they probably did. Parents are only human, after all. If he was any other person on the planet that I spend this much time with and behaves like he does, all other things being equal, I would be yelling at him like 50 percent of the time. Or more. Who else would be allowed to ruin the good towels, lose every jacket he's ever had, whine for forty minutes straight, or make it so I can't sneeze without peeing a little *without* being yelled at? I always think it's a miracle I haven't thrown him out the window. Yet.

From the time we're children we're taught to be rational, kind, courteous people, and just when that's what we might actually *be* . . . we have kids. In what way does that make sense? Trying to be rational with a kid up to—I'm going to say nine because my kid's nine and he still doesn't understand why he can't have his own air horn—up to nine is almost impossible, and that is frustrating. So once in a blue moon I yell. I don't beat him or belittle him or stick him in the basement or make him buy me cigarettes. He eats refrigerators full of food every three days and gets to go on field trips. Frankly, sometimes I think he is a little too confident I'll love him no matter what. But because I yelled *"Stop it"* in his ninth year he won't be a Doctor Without Borders.

Occasionally I wonder what about me my son will pick to complain about when he's older. You know, like when you tell your friends how your parents ruined your life. My parents drank, so I complained about that, for instance. *I* won't play "whale war" with Jack. That's a game where we throw stuffed animals at each other. He makes up ever-changing rules depending on who's winning. But once I got bopped in the face by the shoe of a stuffed bear, so I won't play anymore. Maybe that will be his complaint. Or maybe my yelling *"Stop it"* will be what he tells his friends when they're discussing their bad childhoods. He'll say "I was never the same after that yell." But hopefully he'll never say, "You think that's bad, at least your mom didn't throw you out the window." Fingers crossed.

I'm gonna imagine Jack will realize I'm just a person. Not perfect, but not so bad either. I apologized that night and said that I shouldn't have yelled but I was frustrated. He told me he gets frustrated with me and he doesn't yell, which between you and me and the lamppost isn't so true, but I just said, "I know," and again, "I was wrong to yell," at which point he said he was wrong to yell, too, and he was sorry. He asked why we fight sometimes, and I said because we're strong-willed, which means we both want our way. Then he said he *is* strong and made me feel his muscle. Then we lay in his bed and talked and read a book. Looking at him sleeping I thought, *Well, maybe he won't be poet laureate of the United States; maybe he'll just be someone who can say "I'm sorry" and mean it.* Poetry's overrated anyway.

GO EASY ON THE OLD MAN
Matthew Weiner

WHAT CAN I TELL YOU about my personal battle with breast cancer? Oh, wait a minute, that's next week. This one's about kids. In the interest of bringing you up to date, let me tell you that I have a wife of seventeen years, Linda, and four boys, ages eleven through four. And I hate to admit this, but there are very few other people in the world for whom I have any liking at all. This is mitigated—that means affected negatively in a positive way—by the fact that the cute anecdotes I'm going to tell about my amazing children and wife often feature a horrible creature in them: me. The stories begin in my traditional lifestyle with a man and a woman meeting. I know there are other ways, but ours is old-fashioned. I met Linda and we got married and five years later we got pregnant without much effort. I had a feeling this would be the case because I had impregnated a girl in high school, and I remember that the eventual message that I took away from the experience was *Fuck, that was easy.* It took thirty seconds. Neither of us enjoyed it. We never spoke to each other again. I have noticed, by the way, that with four boys I'm assigned a certain amount of virility, as if my sexual energy determined the gender of my children. And I think about my father, who has two boys and two girls, and I immediately realize that I am more of a man. I don't care if you have fifty girls; you're not even a man compared to me.

Now, I don't know if it was my time of life or my temperament, but at that moment in particular when my children started happening, I was in a strained relationship with my parents. When I say strained, I mean not speaking to each other. I mean my sister called me up and said, "Even murderers talk to their mother on Mother's Day." I'd like to tell you my side of the story, but I will still sound like a dick. Suddenly I realized, as the child was on its way, that I would never have to be a mother. And that's a relief to me, because my mother did not make it look easy. Being a father was something I was going to have to deal with, though, and having a son and then many sons meant the reiteration of a complex problem.

I'll be honest with you, and it may have a relationship to the fact that I've chosen a career, as a TV writer and producer, where I stand in front of a bunch of strangers and talk, but I did not get enough love. It's possible there isn't enough of that kind of love for me. I told you about my wife and children; they deliver. But I obviously need something more. I swore not to become my father. Who, by the way, is a kind, well-mannered man of exceptional education and success and is gifted in the healing arts. He is a doctor of rare and excruciating diseases. His patients come to him hopeless and leave invigorated. I am not a patient. Of course, I have no idea as to the real nature of his fathering skills, because whether I have mentioned it or not, I am oversensitive. So I swore not to become my father, and by that I guess I mean short-tempered, sarcastic, indifferent, narcissistic, and hypocritical. It never occurred to me that these were qualities that I was born with. It's like my wife, Linda—she was born with an ability to attract the most irritating people in the world. I mean really annoying people. People who obsess about tiny shit or say the same thing every time you meet them. People who find a way to insult you and have no idea. Actually it made me think for a moment: *She loves me. Am I one of those people?*

Back to not being my father. My plan of attack was sensitivity, listening, and laying off on the beating the crap out of people. I'll admit it's an effort, especially when they won't fucking listen. Still, I have a pretty spotless record. A couple of shakes, some pinches, maybe a wrist twist, but this is minimal. On a scale of 10 I am at a .005. Now, hitting children is a time-honored tradition, and it has been sustained by the magic of simple logic: Kids get hit, they hate it, they grow up to be adults and do it to kids who hate it. Well, it stops with me. Unlike my father, I use my words. I say things to my kids like "If Grandpa were here right now, he'd be beating the crap out of you." It's intergenerational character assassination, but it gets the job done. *I want to beat you. Grandpa would beat you. But I shan't. So keep your love coming in this direction.*

My oldest son, Marten, had hit his little brother Charlie. Marten was four years old and a thumb sucker. Charlie was two years old, really just a delicious blob of fat that smelled like pee. Anyway, Marten had been sent to bed without dinner. The first and last time I did this. After all, we're talking about Weiner on Weiner violence here. Needless to say, following through on this punishment was excruciating for me. I wanted him to eat dinner. I mean, isn't the whole purpose of a parent to keep a child from feeling pain? And here I was dishing it out Abu Ghraib–style. Lie in bed, feel the hunger pang in the pit of your stomach, and think about how bad you are. It had to be done. And honestly, Grandpa *would* have been beating the crap out of him. But I am a sensitive father. So, of course, eventually I weakened and went to his room.

It would make a better story if I had brought some food, but I didn't. I simply sat on the edge of Marten's bed, in the dark, with a crack of light coming in through the hallway, and I looked at him there, teary-eyed, still sobbing, a little blanket pulled up to his chin, his thumb peeking out and disappearing into his mouth. I said to him, "Do you know what you did wrong?" What a perfect question to ask. God, I know so much more than he does. And he says, sniff, "I shouldn't have hit Charlie." Perfect. I'm done here. But now for some fathering. "What are you feeling?" I ask. He pulls his thumb out of his mouth and says, "My penis." I burst out laughing. Marten joined me, but mostly out of surprise. He did not know what was funny. Cute story, right? Adorable child. I don't even come off that bad in this one. I'm just an oversensitive twentieth-century male concerned about feelings.

I'd take that cliché. I'd really like to. But...One day, we were going on a car trip. I had an Audi A6, which I now can honestly say I loved like a child. The two boys were in the backseat, and we were going to Yosemite. We weren't staying at the Ahwahnee, if you were wondering. We were eating at the Ahwahnee. We were staying at the Wawona, which is beautiful in its own right. But if you think you are staying in Yosemite there, you're insane. You have to drive twenty-five minutes on this vomitty road to see all the Germans and their black socks and sandals. Which is why I go. We have two car seats (we're law-abiding), a double stroller, diapers, ass wipes, three bags, winter coats, and a grocery bag filled with chocolate milk, Ritz crackers, and string cheese, which my kids don't eat but we keep buying. Now, I don't want groceries in my car, so I take the bag full of food, which I had assumed being on vacation I would buy in small increments in restaurants, and I put it in the trunk. The A6 has an amazing trunk. It's carpeted. If some Mafia guy were to throw you in a trunk, you'd pick this one. I put the groceries in the trunk, and it's packed. And I try to close the top. And I can't. I push down on it hard. Then I start slamming. And with each slam, I curse. "Mother. Fucker. God. Damn. Mother. Fucking. Son (of a) Bitch." Finally I got it closed, but I didn't trust it. I thought I might have just broken it into closing, so I pressed the button on the key. And it popped open with a perfect click. It was closed. I'm such a fool. Now I have to do it again. Well, at least I know it's possible. So I start slamming again. And you know the end of the story. I didn't stop until the spare tire well was filled with chocolate milk. However, this was one mess in the car I can honestly say wasn't my fault. I confronted Linda with what she had done. And I realized I might not have become the father my father was, but I certainly was the husband.

The trunk scene touched some emotion inside of me, and from that moment on, without warning, that man would come out. It's hard to gauge what's the worst offense. Marten asked for a cell phone, and I said no. He said, "But I want one." I said,

"You don't need a phone and you don't want a phone. Every time the phone rings, it invites trouble into your life. Every time the phone rings, it's something bad." Marten said, "All my friends have one." I said, "Well, that's great, then I'll know how to reach you. I'll call your friends." My father's reasoning.

Charlie, my nine-year-old, remarked that he was puzzled about why he had to listen to adults. I said to him, "I'm going to give you ten dollars and whatever you want from the house, and you can go out and live on the streets. Take the subway. Let's see how you do on your own. I'll find you crying in the gutter." My father's sense of justice.

Then there was the moment I actually heard my father's voice coming out of my mouth. He's alive, so there's nothing mystical about it. Marten had to have dental surgery. While coming out of the anesthetic, he sat and sobbed, trying to catch his breath. Linda had reached him a few minutes before me from the waiting room. Fine, I was in the bathroom. Just 'cause your kid's having surgery doesn't mean you can't go to the bathroom. I asked, "What's wrong?" My wife said, "The doctor said this is how they react to the anesthetic. It's a release." Now my beautiful baby is crying so I curl up next to him on the La-Z-Boy. He's inconsolable, but I try. In fact I start stroking his hair, even though I empathically know it's bothering him. Just then, Dr. Dentist approaches. I call him that to hide his real name, because he is a dick. He observes my son crying and says, "Huh. The boys don't usually do that." I sit there stunned at this callous insinuation that my son is . . . feminine. He whips out his prescription pad, clicks his free pen, which he probably removed recently from between the breasts of some drug rep, and says Marten will need antibiotics. "There's the pill and there's the liquid. I think he can take the pill." Linda strokes

Marten's leg through the ratty airline blanket. "He'll take the liquid," she says. I say, "He can take the pill." And I say it with such force that the discussion is actually over. Linda shoots me a look, but Dr. Hair Transplants writes a prescription for pills.

We pick up the pills on the way home, and now we're in the kitchen. Marten is standing next to me, quite together. I hand him a big white gelatin pill. He puts it in his mouth, takes a sip from a big glass of water, and swallows. It's still there. I tell him it might take a few tries. He tries again. He's blinking a lot, so I know he's trying. Finally I suggest one large gulp of water to power it down. He fills his cheeks up like Dizzy Gillespie. Swallows hard. Now he's angry like it's my problem. He says it's still there. Now the gelatin is dissolving, and I can tell that it tastes terrible. As I fill the glass, I tell him to make a continuous flow of normal drinking and it will wash the pill down. He starts drinking, followed by gagging and fake throw-up sounds. Okay, maybe real throw-up sounds. And I yell at him, "Just drink water the way a person drinks water." I swear to you *I* didn't say that. "A person." I think it's a New York thing. Both of my parents use this term to refer to all acceptable behavior. What kind of a person does that?

I know what you're all wondering. He did swallow the pill. Or you're wondering how I allowed my masculinity to be attacked so indirectly. No, you're wondering why I'm telling you this. Short-tempered, sarcastic, indifferent, narcissistic, and hypocritical. Oh God, that's who I am. Television writing is social. We dine out on our pain. There's a lot of raincoat opening, too. Parents take a beating. They make good drama. I remember my boss saying to me after one particularly detailed tirade, "Come on, give the old man a break. He made you who you are." I felt guilty because I knew he was right. I get a lot of mileage out of the old man. We try to hide this ugliness from our children, but it's futile. And as they grow, they will recognize we are human beings, and they will hate us for it, maybe even for years, but they will eventually forgive us, maybe even publicly.

WHAT CAN I SAY? I did not become my father. I *am* my father. With the hairy forearms and disciplining other people's children and eating your Halloween candy while you sleep—I'm sick about it. All I can do is try to use my powers for good. My oversensitive one, Arlo, likes to dress up. Not in costumes but in fancy clothes. I'll admit I envy his confidence as he walks around in a top hat and tails and knickers. He got to meet Alice Cooper, and they were mutually grooving on each other. At school, though, when he was five, some older kid says to him one morning, "Why do you dress like that? Why do you do that?" It's hard to explain what wasn't nice about it unless you are oversensitive like Arlo and me. Arlo's eyes well. So I say to the eight-year-old, "Why are you so boring? It's sad, but you are. Why is that?" As we walked away, Arlo smiled and grabbed my hand. And when you humiliate another child to make yours feel better, that's good parenting.

STOP LICKING THE WALL

Beth Harbison

"I AM COMPLETELY SERIOUS, TAKE the trash can off your head *now*."

We were staying in an ornate suite in the New York Palace Hotel, which contained a glass-shelved bar and lots of fussy, fragile knickknacks. My eight-year-old daughter had decided it would be fun to put a wastebasket on her head—a wastebasket that God-knows-how-many strangers had dropped, blown, spat, or otherwise expelled God-knows-what into—and walk around, a veritable bowling ball in a nine-hundred-dollars-a-night-plus-damages bowling alley.

It wasn't the first time I'd been amazed at the things I'd said in the interest of educating and protecting my children.

"Don't run with scissors"? "Don't play with matches"? Those ordinary gems were for other moms.

Moms with *normal* children.

For me, it was "Stop wiping your nose on the dog!"

"When I say get out of the pool to pee, I don't mean on the sidewalk!"

"Changing your name to Superman does *not* give you the ability to fly, don't *ever* try that again!"

"Don't put the wheels from your Hot Wheels cars in your ears."

Did you ever wonder who the idiot was that Petula Clark had to instruct not to sleep in the subway? Not to stand in the pouring rain?

I'm guessing he was a Harbison.

Once upon a time—and, believe me, it is a fairy-tale remembrance for me—I used to talk to other grown people about grown-up things. I could converse about politics, art, almost anything, without looking out the corner of my eye for sparks, fire, blood, or accidental drownings in toilet bowls.

Then I had children. Two of them, a girl and a boy, born ten years—and two miscarriages—apart. I have been at this for a *long* time. With the first one I was young and feeling my way through an unexpected pregnancy; raising a baby at twenty-two was a bit like being a finger-wagging bossy older sister. In retrospect—back in the quaint days when the counter clerk at the airport would simply ask you if a swarthy-looking man with a bomb and an agenda had packed your suitcase—the world was a lot safer. But watching my baby cross my living room that was strewn with Duran Duran CDs, John Hughes Betamax tapes, and baby clothes felt like watching her swim a length of shark-infested ocean. "Watch out!" "Be careful!" "Slow down!"

The world changed a lot during the decade that passed before the next baby was born; the Internet became easy and accessible, cell phones became the norm, TiVo made life wonderful. We entered a new millennium and the world got smaller, more intimate. And briefly—this was 2000—it felt a little safer.

With information on almost anything just a few clicks away, and cell phones cheap enough to give to my children and sophisticated enough to contain locators, I foolishly thought having a second child would be easier. I certainly thought that I'd be more relaxed, that I'd worry less, that everything would fall more naturally into place. Because micromanagement and constant instruction—and the accompanying constant worry—tend to be the domain of the *new* parent, right?

Not in my case. If I'd kept my mouth shut and let my son put tiny rubber wheels in his ears unchecked, I'd probably be giving him these directives in sign language.

With both children it was the same. Those first few tentative, failed baby steps were precious. We gloried in them. Encouraged them. Pulled the children along with sheer will, clapping and shouting encouragement like we were cheering on a Super Bowl win.

They were brilliant. The smartest children ever. Raising them would be like having the most witty, entertaining houseguests in the world.

Then we spent the next two years chasing around what amounted to a two-foot drunk issuing instructions that only someone very drunk, very stupid, or completely inexperienced with life could need.

"Stop licking the wall."

"That's a birdbath, not a toilet. Apologize to Mr. Palmer and get a bag."

"It's pronounced *pum*kin, honey, not *fuck*in. Please don't tell Mrs. Clemens you saw her *fuckin* in the window of her front room last night."

I used to use this mouth to discuss global warming, the "Francis Bacon was really Shakespeare" theory, the works of Hemingway, and, okay, I'll admit it, *Big Brother* and *Survivor*.

Now I say things that would make no sense to a foreigner trying to learn English.

"Stop putting green beans in your brother's nose."

My parting instructions when I leave my kids at their friends' houses have become embarrassing. "Play nicely. Share. Don't pull the dog's whiskers out. Knock before entering the bathroom. Don't put a Ping-Pong ball in your mouth to see if you can whistle with a Ping-Pong ball in your mouth. Look both ways before crossing the street, and that means side to side not up and down. Please don't talk to Mrs. X about the president again. In the unlikely event that it seems like a good idea for you to stick your peanut butter and jelly sandwich to the underside of the kitchen table, please don't."

Every time I think I've covered every possible scenario, no matter how illogical, they find a previously undiscovered loophole and I have to add something like "Don't wipe snot on the wall while you're sitting on the toilet" to the list.

It's not always entirely their fault. Sometimes I forget my children take everything literally, so a metaphor gets me into trouble. When my father died just before my daughter's eighth birthday, I assured her that, even though he was gone, he would always be with her.

She didn't sleep for days.

Finally I had to backtrack and say something that made more sense to her, even though it felt less true to me.

"He's gone and we'll miss him."

It fell short of the spiritual lesson I wanted to take the opportunity to impart, but ultimately I believe it spared her the nightmarish imaginings of her grandfather standing by in the dark, unmoving, unspeaking, uncomprehending. Not quite himself, not quite gone.

We'd taken our cue from an earlier problem, when my husband had tried to explain the importance of hand washing in order to remove potentially dangerous germs. Now, I will say I think he probably overstated the case. He tends to lose patience when forced to argue over simple instructions and I'm fairly sure that argument ended with something like, "Because if you don't wash your hands, you might eat germs that will make you get sick and die!"

I didn't actually *hear* him say it but, given the fact that she turned into Lady Macbeth, washing her hands into a cracked and bleeding mess for the next several months until she finally got enough therapy to stop, makes me think his argument was pretty compelling.

That's why when my son had to be told not to lick the wall, I explained, simply, that he might get a bad stomachache. Children get too obsessed with more dramatic ideas. No one gets obsessed with the idea of puking or diarrhea.

The other day, it was like the third day of summer vacation and my son was getting bored, and I heard my daughter say, "Oh, my God, Jack, take the trash can off your head!" I swear to God, it's true. And I took a moment to appreciate the sweet irony of her incredulity but, of course, it wasn't *her* kid who was grinding the remnants of bathroom waste into his hair, it was mine.

So the sweet irony dissolved like smoke and I had to Handle

the Situation while she walked out of the room, rolling her eyes at his stupidity.

This could have been a good place to point out that they outgrow the need for this sort of obvious instruction, that as children grow older they also grow wiser and the advice turns to a more poignant, more meaningful "neither a borrower nor a lender be" kind of thing. You might imagine—or at least I would have—that by the time my daughter was eighteen, we'd be having deep talks about relationship decisions, career directions, coping with changing friends and deepening responsibilities.

But, no. Two days before she called her brother an idiot for putting a trash can on his head, I'd had to tell her, "It's not my job to remind you that you're a vegetarian before you start pulling meat off a rotisserie chicken carcass and scarfing it down," because she "Could. Not. Believe." I had stood by and watched that when yesterday she'd told me meat was gross and she was never eating it again.

I cannot even imagine what I'll have to say next. Will I be the one responsible for telling my grandchildren an umbrella is not a parachute? Am I the one who will have to call Poison Control if they pour themselves juice cups full of orange cough medicine, thinking it's juice? At this rate, will my children even be capable of *having* their own kids one day without explicit and inappropriate instruction from me?

I don't know if the fault is mine, if there was something I could have said very early on that would have blanketed everything from eating Barbie hair to bringing the wading pool into the house. Do Aesop's Fables cover this kind of thing? Would reading them "The Donkey and the Lap Dog" subconsciously communicate basic common sense to them in a way that real life apparently didn't?

All I know is that I'm not alone. My friend's son stuck Snaus-ages on the trays at a party one time and she didn't know it until she found the half-eaten ones all around the house the next day. There's something you wouldn't have thought you'd have to say to the kids during party prep beforehand!

Just the other day, I heard a mother at the neighborhood pool say to her toddler, "Just put your shorts on your head and *stop whining.*" I looked over at them and the reason for *needing* the shorts on the head wasn't obvious, but I knew there had to be a good reason.

There always is.

So I'll just chug along, trying to keep my family alive and healthy, occasionally doling out more of these bizarre words of common sense. "I don't care how it looks, the toilet is *not* filled with blue Kool-Aid. Now pour out this drink you gave me and get mommy her happy juice."

THE TENNIS PRO

Neal Pollack

ON FRIDAYS, ELIJAH MEETS HIS friends in the park to play sports. They have a private coach, it costs eight bucks, and he gets to learn the fundamentals of various games without us having to deal with the agony of defeat. Heaven forfend that a contemporary child should experience loss or disappointment.

One of Elijah's favorite things about the park is the preponderance of tennis balls in the bushes. There are courts all around, and stray balls often pop up in unforeseen places. He likes to gather abandoned balls and then bring them home so our dog can chew the hell out of them.

Yesterday, after a spirited hour of T-ball, Elijah and I walked back to the car. I already had four tennis balls stuffed into his glove, but he wanted more. He walked along the edge of the main court's fence and found one in the shrubbery.

"That's enough," I said.

"One more!" he said. He stuck his hand through a hole in the fence and tried to pull one out.

"It's not gonna happen," I said.

I could see manipulative tears, signifying disappointment, build in his eyes. He walked along the fence, trying to magically extract a ball from underneath. Finally, we came to the gate opening. There was a ball two inches away from the opening.

"Stick your hand through there and get one," I said.

When we turned the corner, there was a guy with a scraggly beard, a bandanna, and messy blond-brown hair pulled back into a ponytail. He wore sunglasses and sat there with his arms crossed.

"Hello," I said.

He wagged his fingers as if he wanted me to give him something. His lips were pursed. He held a tennis racket. Whoops.

I started tossing him the balls.

"Don't give them all away, Daddy!" Elijah said.

"That's it, tough guy," said the tennis pro. "Hand 'em over."

"I—"

"Is that what you do?" he asked. "Teach your child to steal?"

"No!" I said. "I'm sorry. I didn't think there was anyone on the court—"

"I didn't think there was anyone on the court," he said snidely.

"Hey, listen, buddy."

"Hey, *you* listen, buddy," he said. "Why don't you learn how to be a decent dad?"

Now, I was wrong to tell Elijah to take that tennis ball, but it really was an innocent mistake. Besides, teaching my child to steal? Who was I? Fagin? Would I really tell my son that he's got to pick a pocket or two? My blood began to bubble.

"You know what, man?" I said. "I hope if you have kids someday, someone talks to you like this."

"I do have kids," he said. "And I raise them right. Unlike you."

Well, that was it.

"*You sonofabitch!*" I screamed. "*You motherfucking bastard! How dare you talk to me like that?*"

A middle-aged Mexican woman was walking into the parking lot with her daughters. I pointed to Elijah.

"Watch him," I said to her, and I bolted for the fence. I was halfway up before she got to me and started pulling me down.

"Don't do it!" she said. "We're all bad parents! None of us know what we're doing!"

This was true, of course, but I wasn't chilled yet.

"After what he said to me?" I said, and I shouted toward him again, "*Fuck you, you fat asshole!*"

"It's not worth it," she said. "Look at your boy."

Elijah was standing against the fence, arms crossed, saying, "Hmph."

"Do you really want him to see you fight another man?" she asked.

"No," I said sheepishly.

"I can tell you're a good daddy," she said. "Look at him. He's so cute. He's clean."

I looked at him. He was definitely cute, but he'd been rolling around in diamond dirt for an hour, and he was absolutely filthy. So the one piece of evidence she had of me as a good parent was completely false. *Wait,* I thought, *maybe she's an unreliable narrator! Maybe I* should *go fight this guy!*

I moved toward the fence again.

"He can't talk to me like that," I said.

"No, he can't," she said, "but he did anyway. Besides, you were wrong, too."

She winked at me as she said this. Was she flirting with me? Anyway, she was right. I'd made a mistake. But I hadn't deserved the lecture.

In the car, Elijah said, "Daddy, why did you call that guy the F-word?"

"Because he was being a jerk," I said.

"You can't use that word, Daddy," he said. "No ice cream for you tonight."

At that moment, I desperately needed ice cream, but I said, "You're right. I'm sorry, son. It's just that he said mean things to me and I got upset."

"It's okay," he said. "I think you're a good daddy. You just lose your temper sometimes."

"No, I don't."

"Yes, you do, like you yelled at me the time I punched you in the peenie."

"I think I should get a pass on that one."

"Or when you yelled at Mommy to stop talking about Barack Obama all the time."

"That was probably wrong of me."

"Or when you threw your sandwich on the floor in the restaurant because they put mayonnaise on it—"

"Okay, okay, I have a temper! So do you."

"I know I do. Sometimes things make me so angry."

"Me, too. So listen, it was wrong for me to tell you to take that tennis ball."

"And it was wrong for that tennis guy to call you a bad daddy."

"Right. No one's perfect."

"That's not true," Elijah said. "Everyone's perfect."

I wanted to counter that with some cynicism, but then I thought better of it. Just because I have no faith in humanity doesn't mean I should make him feel the same way. The world crushes you soon enough, and a good daddy should protect his kids as long as possible.

Of course, he also shouldn't cuss out a skanky tennis pro in public, but nobody's perfect.

READING HER JOURNAL

Anonymous

I HAVE A FOURTEEN-YEAR-OLD DAUGHTER. She's amazing, of course: smart and tall and beautiful (an equestrian!), and learning more about the adult world every day, but still a child in many ways. So while she's taller than I am, has bigger breasts, wears makeup with more aplomb, and reads great authors like Ian McEwan and Camus, she's also obsessed with Batman, giggles at times like a hyena, and can eat a pint of ice cream a day without gaining an ounce. Unlike her little sisters who seem as though they'll always be telling me everything they think/say/feel, Miranda has, since she was tiny, been sort of secretive and slightly aloof, a private girl, a cool girl. There's plenty of emotion there, but she's not wearing it on her sleeve. So as adolescence has come upon us, I've often wondered: How will I know she's safe? Will she tell me if she needs me? What if I miss some big signs of disaster ahead?

I was raised by a bohemian intellectual mother, a black independent filmmaker and playwright who was in her own creative world much of the time and who valued privacy and the written word above much else. I know she loved my brother and me fiercely, but she often had no idea what was going on with us—had no clue I was having sex or smoking pot or sneaking out of the house at night and, probably most painfully, wasn't aware when I was having social problems at school, feeling hurt or left out or being called a slut by my classmates. And then she died when I was nineteen, leaving me in charge of my brother, and as a result of all this and perhaps much more, never in my life have I felt very well taken care of. So of course for me, in the way that we all parent in reaction to the way we were parented, I most desperately want my kids to feel cared for above all else. To know that they are loved and watched at all times. Close but not too close, the eternal parent dilemma.

One day last fall when we were wallpapering Miranda's room (in black velvet, no less) and all her crap was out in the hallway, I decided to be helpful and do some weeding. As I was throwing away all sorts of unnecessary shit, like homework from second grade, melted candy, and ancient tubes of mascara, I came across her diary. Ugh. The temptation. To open or not? What's the right thing to do? How compelling. How delicious, and what an utter invasion of privacy.

I cracked the book open and was immediately drawn in by Miranda's teenage bubble printing, which reminded me of my own at that age, and then by her incredible voice: passionate, poetic, sarcastic, angry at times, often funny. And the stories: the way that teenagers are virtually oblivious to the world outside their own, the way that *boys* dominate everything. It brought me back. But the content, what to do about the content? I learned all sorts of things that afternoon: that she'd been stealing alcohol from my house, getting felt up, and sneaking out at night; her disdain for many of the adults in her life, and her crushes on others; that she'd flirted with bulimia and had a few weeks where food and weight were an incessant theme; how she'd felt wounded for ages by her best girlfriend; endlessly frustrated by one of her siblings in particular; was sick of certain teachers. All in all, pretty normal stuff. But who am I to say what's normal?

The second I began reading, I knew that if I was going to go down this path, I could never use what I learned against her. I told myself I was doing it for her own good, to make sure I didn't miss anything big, like heroin addiction or a teenage pregnancy. There's a lot of truth to that, but as with anything there were other layers of truth. For example, that it was a great read! Up there with *Gossip Girls*, *The A-List*, *The Clique*. Salacious and sexy and funny and shocking at times. And really well written! Even when she insulted me, her mother (as in "My fucking mother thinks *feelings* are more important than anything else. I'm so sick of her!"), it was like a gift from above to know what she's thinking and yes, just an incredible voyeuristic treat to be *in my daughter's own mind*! Don't we all want that?

On top of the entertainment value, reading the diary was useful. And I admit I've done it since, at least three more times. Knowing that she was warming to the idea of throwing up after meals was helpful (and terrifying, yes, but I kept the fear at bay); it made me pay more attention to her eating habits. Knowing she and her friends are drinking was good information; it made me figure out a system of tracking the alcohol in my house. That she's getting closer to being sexually active? Made me bring up protection when we went for her annual physical. Plus, all this gives me stuff to talk about with her, in a general way, not in a specific, accusatory way. And what a relief to know that there's nothing else yet: no cocaine, no correspondence with convicts, no oral sex! No shoplifting, no riding in cars with boys, no alcoholic binges, no cigarettes; there are so many things that could easily, and well might, happen.

I could die early, the way my mother did, and leave her alone. We all, to some extent, replicate the lives of our parents. But our lives also diverge from theirs in huge, unexpected ways, and the line between the two is an endless struggle, a balancing act that our kids have no idea we're performing. As long as I'm around, I'll be here trying to give Miranda all the love and guidance I wish I'd had, and I'll never hold anything she says or does against her. It's all normal; I just want to help if I can. I'm not saying I'm a saint; I get plenty angry when she's nasty or inconsiderate or does stupid things.

What I'm saying is that this particular betrayal, this reading of her private work, written to herself, for herself, will never come back to bite her in the ass. It's much more likely, of course, to bite *me* in the ass, like when she comes across this essay one day, and then I'll tell her that it's my own bad behavior; no justification, just a mom who crossed a line trying to do the right thing. She might hate me in that moment; but one day she may also look back and recall the pleasure of being watched so carefully, of knowing that there's someone in the world who's interested in every stupid/wonderful/graceful/dangerous thing she does and feels.

I FINALLY SWORE AT MY DAUGHTER

Todd Waring

I FINALLY SWORE AT MY daughter the other day. She's thirteen going on Satan. Just so you don't think I'm swearing at a toddler. No, no, I'm swearing at a thirteen-year-old!!

I have sworn *near* her before, as she was leaving the room or had already left the room. Under my breath. Quiet enough so she couldn't hear me. She's got good hearing, too, so I was really chancing it all those times. All those times she really pissed me off. All those times she told me she didn't care what I thought, or said to me, "What are you going to do about it? There's *nothing* you can do about it. You always say you're going to take away TV, but that doesn't last. What are you going to do about it?"

Well, I can swear under my breath as you walk away, but actually hope you catch it as if you weren't supposed to, even though I'm secretly hoping you will, as if somehow it came from someone or something else and you just heard it but couldn't ascribe it to me specifically. I could do that!

Just a side thing here: When they berate you for *not* sticking to the rules that they hate, what is that? Just knee-jerk opportunism. It's like a guy being flogged on a pirate ship going, "You skipped one, lame-o!" Anyway . . .

It took me a while to really figure out what I was doing when I was sending these bombs out into the ether. I know I felt better saying them. It feels real good. It's wrath. It's one of the seven deadly sins. Wrath.

As I look back on it, though, I knew I didn't want her to think these stealth bombs actually came from me. I don't think there's a word for that kind of talking. You know, other than the catch-all "passive-aggressive." But I think that applies more to hoping that the person *does* know where the insane attack is coming from. No, this was more like you want them to hear it, but you don't want them to know where it's coming from. I guess it's ventriloquism. Ventriloquism-talking.

Yeah, I was trying to hang it in the air somewhere and hope she'd just walk into it, anonymously. Bump her head on it and assess it in a positive, self-help kind of way. "I'm a fucking asshole. Hmm. I'll have to look into that." Oh, that was the gem.

This was all unexamined until one day I let it fly with her right there. (Though I did turn away as I said it!) The scene was this: It's the morning, on a school day. My daughter has already skipped her first class. Which is another story. It's "AMPE," morning gym class, a kind of Guantánamo for tweeners. It starts at 7:30 A.M., so I have a certain amount of sympathy. We won't go into how many *times* she's skipped AMPE, just mention it to let you know sympathy has limits. So it's now 8:30 and we're moving past PE and quickly into first period. I am in my office writing a note for school about the lateness. Perjuring myself for my daughter.

What is the late note, anyway, but collusion in the joint cover-up of failure? "Dear Mr. Gropner, My child and I agree that we have failed in the simple act of getting her ass to school on time. Please accept this excuse (whatever I have down here) as some thin veil of officialdom to cover our inadequacy." And the school does the same. "Yes, we accept your handwritten lies as proof of your vigilant parenting, and will join you yet again in this ritual of phony concern."

I'm writing the note, and she comes in. "Where's my green jacket?" "There's a laundry basket in the living room. Maybe it's in there," I attempt to say. I get as far as "laundry basket" when *"I wouldn't put it in the laundry!!"* comes shooting out.

Lordy-may, there's so much in that moment. We all know that, in and of itself, a flare-up like that isn't enough to pre-cipitate the nuclear option. We also know that the nuclear op-tion is never the result of calm reflection.

I'm writing you a note (a complete fabrication) on your behalf, so you can slip back into school with as little fuss as possible. You've asked me to help you locate a jacket that you never put away prop-erly anyway. Then, when I offer a suggestion, you bite my head off.

What do I do? What does one do? "Honey, that's a hurtful tone." I can't even begin to see my way to that kind of even-handed response because of the blood that's filling up my eye sockets. No response is a very good choice and probably what would have been the best approach. Y'know, when *they* get that last word and it's one of those outrageously ugly comments, it just sits there ringing in the air untainted by anything I add; that's all they can hear. That's when she can hear herself as others do. That's when she learns. And that's—not what happened here.

No. What happened was something different. What happened was, I turned away from her and muttered, "Fucking asshole." I swore at her. I didn't raise my voice. I was calm. I wanted it to sink in. *You should know, you're being a fucking asshole. Neutral statement.* Then I waited. What's she going to do? She hates swearing, it's truly offensive to her. She's a highly sensitive—and still somewhat innocent—fucking asshole.

Well. She stood there silently, reached out her right hand, and without looking cleared off a shelf of books and pictures onto my wife's desk and onto the floor. Then, before I could say anything, she walked down the hall, clearing another shelf as she went.

Pretty effective.

Now what? I didn't respond to the shelf clearing. What's to say? "You fucking asshole"? I had raised that point earlier. And she made her point. Which is: There's nothing you can do that I can't match. Good. But how do you get the genie back in the bottle? Now there's nuclear waste everywhere, and who's going to clean it up?

I finished up the note. She found her jacket. We're about to go to the car and she says, "I'm sorry about the stuff."

I wasn't expecting that. I just scorched her tender little asshole ears and she apologizes first. I thought we were in for a long cold war. Slamming doors and terse replies. Rejected attempts at reconciliation. Perhaps worst of all, having to explain all this to my wife. How the morning went, the note, the jacket, the nasty comment, the moment, the F-bomb, the shelf-bomb. How the whole thing got out of control and how I blew it. Then I realized she felt she had dropped the big one, too. That she'd crossed a line and felt bad. I shot right back with an apology of my own. "I shouldn't have used those words. I know how bad it sounds." "No, I shouldn't have snapped at you." "Thanks, honey. I'm really sorry." Then it . . . went away.

And stayed away. And never came back.

My daughter's not a fucking asshole. But sometimes she's *very* good at hiding it.

MY ALMOST MAN

Caroline Aaron

WE HAVE ALL READ THE books; we are all motivated to be good parents. We know we are only custodians for a while. They don't belong to us; they are only entrusted to us. From the first time they roll over they are in the process of separating. It is our job to encourage them to go from dependence to independence. Blah blah blah—well, it is all bullshit, because when they really are leaving, it is so inconceivable, so wrenching, and so unimaginable.

I am racing to the door—he is so far ahead of me—I have to reach it before he walks out. How did he get so far ahead when I was in the lead for so long? I am winded, I am spent, and I can't outrun him. I scream instead—hoping my voice will close the distance—"There is still so much I have to teach you, there is still so much I have to tell you." He is searching for his keys—a delay, I gain on him—"Civil disobedience!" I holler. "What?" he says, uninterested. "Did I tell you to object when the world is wrong and you are right?" "Uh-huh. Mom, have you seen my keys?" I have, but I will be damned if I tell him where they are. "Ben, wait up, I need to talk to you!" "I have to go, Mom." "Where are you going?" "Out"—he finds his keys—I am running out of time. "Ben?" "What?" he says impatiently with his hand on the doorknob—I have to cut to the chase—"Uh, how's your inner life?" "I'm good," he says, and he is gone. I look out the portal window of the front door. He is on his cell phone, laughing and slipping into the driver's seat. Who is he talking to, and why is he in the driver's seat that has always been my seat, not his?

He's a boy. The books say it is natural for him to withhold from us; he is separating, becoming his own person, forming his own opinions. Separating, becoming his own person, forming his own opinions? How ridiculous! Those books don't know shit. Your opinions are my opinions. What else would they be, because you are me, aren't you? You're my child, you belong to me. Why does your being older change that? It doesn't, not to me, maybe to you. Well, guess what, buster, you're not the only person in this equation, and I am here to tell you that you cannot separate from me *ever*!

Ben's car has rounded the corner and he is out of sight. I go over to my desk. I sit down to re-revise his college application essay for the umpteenth time. I have other things to do, but we have to get the essay down to 500 words—we are currently at 609. You see, my son is applying to college, or, more accurately, Ben and I are applying to college, with the assumption that Ben will be the only one going.

Applying to college—no matter what you have heard about

it, it is so much worse. It is a horrible process. In addition to the four AP classes he must take his senior year to demonstrate his appetite for intellectual challenge, he also has test prep, essays to write, endless meetings with college counselors, envelopes to address, and teachers to solicit for recommendations. Then there is the nail biting while waiting for the scores and then more test prep to see if he can ratchet up those numbers a hundred points or so. Plus community service hours to cram in to demonstrate what a well-rounded fellow he is. I fluctuate between feeling incredibly sorry for the stress he is under and rage at the fact that I am enlisted in any way. Why am I editing your essay? Fuck you, Ben, *you* do it. If you are so anxious to be your own person, then go ahead and do it. Ace your classes, complete your applications, hang out with your friends, and have a life private and separate from me. Oh, good, we are at 539 on the word count. I call him. He doesn't pick up. I leave a message. "Ben, could you call me and tell me if there is any wiggle room on this word count? We are down to 539."

How come when I call he doesn't pick up but when it's any of his friends he answers on the first ring? It's like he has supersonic hearing when it's one of his posse. No matter what the noise level, he hears that phone. I am always amazed. I call him back and leave another message. "When are you coming home from being out? I need to do this with you. Come home." I hang up and say "please" out loud to myself. "Come home, please." It is December already. I only have until August, only six more months to load his hard drive. He came downstairs the other morning and said, "I was just thinking this might be the last year I ever live at home. Cool."

We are in countdown mode. Every day now I wonder what it will be like when he is gone. I cannot imagine how it will feel to still feel him as part of my every waking thought and not have a presence to go with those thoughts. What a gyp, I think. We put all this work into them, when they are incapable and incompetent, when they are lost, when they are unformed; we do all the heavy lifting. We give them the tools to be capable, we educate them so they can be in the world, we give them direction, we give them values, we give them time and love, and when our handiwork starts to take shape and you go, *I really like this person—my child—*the one who went from a mewling helpless infant to this really interesting cool funny smart charming almost-man, and you think, *I would like to hang out with you, not surprisingly you are my kind of person, I think it would be fun to spend time with you.* Well, the timing is off, all fucked up. Just when they might be people you would want to spend time with is the exact same time they leave. What a monster rip-off.

Why is this so upsetting? It's not like Ben hasn't been away, and for large chunks of time. Of course, the fishing line has gotten longer as he has grown older, but I still have him hooked on to me. If I ever need to reel him in, I am still holding the rod. Even a few weeks ago, traveling back from the official college visit, I am loitering in airport stores and he looks around to see where I am. He is holding his own boarding pass; he can go right to the gate and sit. He really doesn't need to wait for me, but he still does out of habit. He rushes me; he is annoyed; why am I taking so long! I could tell him, "Go ahead, you don't need me. Just go to the gate and I'll meet you there." But I don't. He will find out soon enough he doesn't need me anymore.

I am not interested in that bullshit that they need you in a new way. I want him to need me in the old way. I want him to need me to feed him and pat him to sleep at night. I want him to need me to transfer him from the stroller to the crib without waking him. I want him to need me to take off my sweatshirt and give it to him because he's cold. I want him to need my ice cream cone because his scoop slipped out when he wasn't looking. I want him to need me to laugh at his jokes and to clap after his made-up skits that are so boring and go on forever. I want him to need to talk to me about movies and music and just nothing because he dug hanging out with me that day. I want him to need me at all his games. I want him to need to stomp away from me when I have been unbearably stupid about what he is trying to say. I want him to need my permission and watch him campaign to get it with the finesse of a successful politician, when I was going to say yes anyway. And I want him to always give me a Christmas list of what he wants that ends with "and some surprises."

I want a do-over. I want to do this job again but in a different way. My goals have changed. I do not want to raise an independent self-confident happy person. Why would I go to all the trouble of basically ruining my life, my career, my body, and my marriage to raise a child who leaves? That is madness. In my do-over, Ben's self-esteem is off the table. I would begin by making him scared of almost everything. I would convince him that he is allergic, and not just to every conceivable food but also to dust. And since dust is everywhere, "You'd better not wander too far away from your dust-free house." Of course, I am now obligating myself to clean, but it is a small price to pay for a grown-up child who is afraid to go out. And I will never make the mistake of saying, "Try to do it yourself. You can do it. I have confidence in you." Or "What do you think?" Or "I am interested in your opinion." Or "What you want is what's important." Or "If you like it is what counts; it isn't important how I feel." Or even "What color would you like your room to be?" And I would never ever say "it's your life" at the beginning of *any* sentence. In my new version of Motherhood it is not relevant how you feel, what your opinions are, what you are capable of, or even what your own taste is. No, you are entirely an extension of me. I am going to write a new parenting book titled *How to Cripple Your Children to Keep Them Eternally Dependent and at Home.*

The door opens, and Ben is back. He blows upstairs and calls down, "Did you finish, Mom?" "Didn't you get my message?" "Oh yeah, I think that's fine." "Well, can you read it? I think it's really good." "I'll read it later. I don't have time now." "What are you doing?" "Oh, I just came home to shower, and then I'm going out again." I am about to yell at him when he adds, "Thanks, Mom, for helping."

Here is the conundrum. If I hadn't raised him to be himself and let who he was emerge over these very short eighteen years, then I might not be so in love with the man he almost is and I might not be so heartbroken that he is growing up and ready to move on.

NOT ENOUGH GOOD OLD DAYS

Dani Klein Modisett

"WHAT'S THIS FANCY ENVELOPE?" I ask Gideon, my seven-month-old, as I spoon vegetable mush into his mouth. I decided to open the mail this morning between swallows because even though caring for an infant in my forties has me so exhausted my head feels numb a lot of the day, I still feel compelled to multitask. My new favorite tandem activities are checking e-mail on my phone while breast-feeding, when I'm not busy making dinner while wearing my child as a hiking accessory.

Gideon opens his mouth like a blond bird begging for more grubworms. I give him a lump of squash while I slide my thumb underneath the seal of what appears to be an invitation. I think, *But no one we know is getting married.*

"TWENTY-FIVE YEARS STRONG," THE RAISED print an-
nounces.

Oh my God, my high school reunion. Twenty-five years? Is
that possible?

"Bring your kids, fun for all," it says underneath.

"Fun for all?" Blech. I guess "Fun for everyone except those
of you who risk reliving being gonged at the high school Gong
Show, and years of sitting home eating ice cream on the couch
while other people were having sex in the back of cars" was too
many words.

And of course it doesn't say "Bring your babies."

Because who has a baby twenty-five years after graduating
from high school? Other than me and my in-vitro fertilization
support group. I'm pretty sure no one else in there went to
Staples High School.

I give Gideon more yellow pabulum and dial my sister.

"THERE'S NO WAY I'M GOING to this," I tell her. I'm so excited to
have a child who's eating vegetables I try stuffing one more
bite in Gideon's mouth. Unfortunately, he's moved on to chew-
ing the strap of his chair. Drool is streaming down the front of
his Onesie.

"Why not?" she asks. I can almost hear the wineglass in her
hand. She's a card-carrying member of the "it's five o'clock
somewhere" club and has been since she got drunk and threw
up on the dance floor in seventh grade. "Fuck them. Go! You
can show off your beautiful family to all those people who
thought you'd never settle down."

"I'm forty-four. With an infant," I say. "I'm a circus freak to them. Again."

"Who cares? And show off those big nursing boobs, too!" She takes another sip. "Listen, you can't dodge high school memories forever, my dear. Wait till the *boys* are in high school."

"I'll be eighty by then," I joke, "and hopefully senile."

I HANG UP AND LOOK over at Gideon, the front of his shirt now soaked. With his pudding-like cheeks, white-blond hair, and saucer blue eyes, he looks like a Gerber baby someone tried to drown for being too cute.

"I won't really be eighty when you graduate high school, buddy, don't worry," I say, pulling him out of his high chair. "I'll be..." I'm not good with math. Never have been. It's no secret I flirted my way through high school physics. "Sixty-three, I'll be sixty-three," I blurt, pulling a diaper off the nearby stack.

"Will you still need me, will you still feed me, when I'm sixty-three?" I sing, trying to lighten the weight of this realization. Gideon giggles at the sight of me shaking my head from side to side.

I smile back, sigh, and think, *Baby penises are really small.*

I fasten the diaper at his hips.

I wonder if it will get proportionately larger as he gets bigger.

I hope it does.

I wonder what other women will think of his penis.

I wonder if I will live long enough to meet any of these women who will evaluate my son's penis.

Will I live to meet his wife?

If he waits as long as I did, it's not looking likely.

WHILE I CONTINUE TO DRESS Gideon for his nap and settle him in his crib, my life flashes forward like animation cels. There I am at his bar mitzvah, closing in on sixty. I'm wearing some Eileen Fisher outfit with no waistband. Unlike the ubiquitous younger mommies in their Hard Tail yoga pants, my body didn't bounce back. In fact, there hasn't been much bouncing in the last ten years, just a lot of hanging. I am standing next to my earnest son witnessing him becoming a man, a doting, wrinkled mommy blob in soft separates.

FIVE YEARS LATER WE'RE AT his high school graduation. Carloads of families pull up to the big day with surfboards and water skis strapped to their hoods. As soon as the ceremony ends, they are heading for sun-and-surf celebratory vacations. The audience is filled with tan, beaming faces. Not me. I'm holding the program up against my nose because I've forgotten my reading glasses in the car, right next to my calcium supplements. During the valedictory speech, I loudly unwrap and chomp on mints to mask the odor of my acid reflux. The ceremony ends, and Gideon throws his cap to me. I reach for it and throw my back out. I hobble to the car wincing, very proud of him, but hoping I can stay awake to watch *American Idol: Where Are They Now?*

THEN I'M AT GIDEON'S COLLEGE graduation. Again I'm in the audience, only this time I can't sit still. If I don't find a bathroom soon I am going to wet the seat. Gideon's girlfriend's mother is trying to tell me where the nearest restroom is, but I can't hear her over the din of the school band because I refuse to wear my hearing aid. Part of the problem is the woman's Asian accent, but the truth is I haven't really heard anything clearly since 2023.

NEXT I'M AT HIS WEDDING. A small, quiet girl glides down the aisle next to her father. She is beautiful. Not my type, but if she makes him happy that's all that matters. A gray-haired trollish-looking woman starts down the aisle, but not without a lot of help. No surprise, that troll is me, I can tell by the outfit, more shapeless swathes of fabric. I look like a Keebler Elf in a silk cocoon. So much for the calcium supplements; I'm so hunch-backed I can barely walk. In fact, is that a skateboard I'm standing on? Yes, it is. I am being pulled down the aisle like a dried-out apple-face doll on wheels to give the illusion of dignity before being placed in my wheelchair waiting on the aisle. It's pretty humiliating, and yet I've never looked so happy.

I WALK OUT OF THE room to toss Gideon's diaper and go pre-heat the oven. I pass a picture of my father in the hallway.

"What are you worried about?" I hear him ask me. "Old, shmold. Who cares what you look like as long as you're alive?" This from a man who refused any chemo treatments that would make his hair fall out. Which is to say, the vain apple doesn't fall far from the even more vain tree.

His voice follows me into the kitchen. "You should only be so lucky to live that long, sweetheart."

Shit, he has a point. *He* was forty-four when he had me, and he died when I was thirty-three. He never even met Tod, forget about Gideon or my five-year-old, Gabriel. Amid my relentless vanity, there's a piece of me that knows that what I am hearing him say is right. No wonder I looked so happy in that wheelchair. He would have given anything to be at my wedding. In fact, when his will to live was waning, my sister would use my "active" social life as incentive for him to hang in there. "Come on, Dad, you don't really want to die yet. Don't you want to stay alive to meet Dani's next boyfriend?"

I COME BACK TO THE crib and notice the receiving blanket from the hospital where Gideon was born under his pillow. My mind takes another leap and I'm in the hospital with Tod by my side. He's almost a decade younger, so he can still stand. And I guess in my fantasy he hasn't left me for someone more age-appropriate, even though I've been telling him to since our first date. We are there for the birth of our first grandchild. Gideon hands me the baby to hold. I take a long, deep breath.

I made it, I think. *I'm old and shriveled and my daughter-in-law hates me, but I'm here and I'm holding a grandchild.*

I WIPE A SMALL TEAR from my eye, an action that takes me back to my kids' room. Gideon is screaming. His favorite toy, a set of plastic car keys, has dropped out of reach. His cry is ear-splitting. It should bug me, but it's so full of life, in this moment I love it. I want to steal it and put it in a sports-top bottle so I can suck it down thirty years from now.

"Here it is, honey," I say, handing him the toy. "You keep

reaching, sweetie, even when they tell you you can't, that you shouldn't, that the odds are against you, you keep fighting.

"And do what makes you happy!" I add, throwing the invitation in the garbage with a flourish and picking up a laundry basket of clean clothes to fold.

Aha! I've stumbled on a perk of being an older mommy. Look how wise I am!

I lean in and kiss Gideon's nose. "Oh! And don't be afraid to settle down young.

"Younger than your friends," I add, tucking him in.

"Younger than is legal. I'll explain when you're older, honey," I whisper in his tiny ear.

"Sweet dreams."

ABOUT THE CONTRIBUTORS

CAROLINE AARON is a bicoastal actress known to theater, television, and film audiences. She has performed on Broadway multiple times, has appeared in dozens of television shows, and has over fifty films to her credit, most notably as Woody Allen's sister in both *Crimes and Misdemeanors* and *Deconstructing Harry.* She lives in L.A. with her husband, Jamie, her daughter, Sydney, and until recently her son, Ben, who is a freshman attending Colby College in Maine.

ANONYMOUS is a former literary agent living in Brooklyn, New York.

CAROLINE BICKS is an English professor at Boston College. Her work has been heard on NPR and seen at Improv Boston. If you think parenting is tough now, check out her book *Midwiving Subjects in Shakespeare's England.*

JAMES BRALY is the writer and performer of the "gaspingly funny" (*Variety*), "never less than excellent" (*The New York Times*) monologue *Life in a Marital Institution*, which enjoyed a sold-out run in New York City at 59E59 Theater and then transferred Off-Broadway to the SoHo Playhouse. For more information on James, please visit www.jamesbraly.com.

DAN BUCATINSKY is an actor/writer/producer (*All Over the Guy, The Comeback, Lipstick Jungle*) who runs the Is Or Isn't Entertainment company with business partner Lisa Kudrow. His partner in life for sixteen years is writer/director Don Roos. They live in Los Angeles and have two children, Eliza and Jonah.

KELL CAHOON has worked on a number of television shows, including *The Larry Sanders Show, NewsRadio,* and *King of the Hill*. He is currently writing for *Psych* and commutes to L.A. every week from Austin, Texas, where he lives with his wife and two sons.

CHRISTY CALLAHAN has worked, in order of length of time spent, as a waitress, movie studio executive, TV writer, script reader, assistant to unpleasant publicist, temp, timeshare salesperson, babysitter, dishwasher, catsitter, Broadway usher, housecleaner, lifeguard, and cook on a yacht (was fired instantly but did get paid, so she's counting it).

CINDY CHUPACK has won an Emmy and three Golden Globes for her work as a writer/executive producer of HBO's *Sex and the City*. She is also the author of *The Between Boyfriends Book: A*

Collection of Cautiously Hopeful Essays. For more information on Cindy or her book, visit www.betweenboyfriends.com.

RICK CLEVELAND is an Emmy-winning writer whose credits include *The West Wing, Six Feet Under,* and *Mad Men.* His one-person show *My Buddy Bill* won the Jury Award for Best Solo Performance at the 2006 HBO Aspen Comedy Festival and debuted on Comedy Central. He is the proud father of Clara, Gus, and Charlie.

MERRIN DUNGEY is a comedian and actress best known for her roles on *Alias* and *The King of Queens.* Her favorite role is being mom to eight-month-old Maisie Olivia. Merrin is married and lives in Los Angeles.

MIMI FRIEDMAN began writing television to support her need to be clothed, fed, and sheltered. She began her writing career with her longtime partner Jeanette Collins for the sketch comedy show *In Living Color.* Most recently they wrote for the series *Big Love.* They are currently writing an original pilot for HBO.

MO GAFFNEY wrote and performed in the award-winning *Kathy and Mo Show* Off-Broadway and on HBO. She has also appeared on television (*Ab Fab, Mad About You,* etc.) and in movies (*Drop Dead Gorgeous, Happy, Texas,* etc.)

DANA GOULD is a comedian and writer. Among his credits is *The Simpsons,* for which he won an Emmy.

BETH HARBISON is a *New York Times* bestselling author of women's fiction, including *Shoe Addicts Anonymous* and *Hope in a Jar.* She lives near Washington, D.C., with her husband and two children. Visit her at www.bethharbison.com.

PETER HORTON is an actor/writer/director. As an actor he is best known for his role on the series *thirtysomething*; as a director for directing the pilot for *Grey's Anatomy* (he also produced *Grey's Anatomy* during its first three years), and as a writer for his six-part limited series *Infidelity* and various political pieces for the *Los Angeles Times* and other publications. His proudest and most profound claim is that he's Lily Ann and Ruby Jane's dad.

MARK HUDIS, former executive producer of *That '70s Show* and *Miss/Guided*, is a measly five feet, five inches tall. How sad is that?

MELANIE HUTSELL played Jan Brady, Tori Spelling, and a demonic Tri Delt girl on *SNL* in the early nineties. Now married with two children, she still performs as much as possible, most notably as a dead ringer for Paula Deen. She is also a screenwriter.

DEBORAH COPAKEN KOGAN is the bestselling author of the memoir *Shutterbabe*, novel *Between Here and April*, and a soon-to-be-released book of essays, *Hell Is Other Parents*. Her writing has appeared in such publications as *The New Yorker* and *The New York Times*, her photographs have been seen in *Newsweek, Time, Photo*, and *GEO*, and she was an Emmy-winning television producer for *ABC News* and *Dateline NBC*. She lives in New York with her husband, three children, and a not-quite-housetrained puppy.

ANDREW MCCARTHY is a contributing editor at *National Geographic Traveler* magazine. For the past twenty-five years he has also been an actor and more recently a director.

CHRISTIE MELLOR wrote *The Three-Martini Playdate, The Three-Martini Family Vacation,* and *Were You Raised by Wolves? Clues to the Mysteries of Adulthood,* for which she received enthusiastic reviews from dozens of publications, including *Newsweek, People,* and the London *Times.* She lives in Los Angeles with her husband and two boys. For more details, visit her Web site at www.christiemellor.com.

JASON NASH is a comedian and actor who cohosts his very funny podcast Guys With Feelings (www.guyswithfeelings.com).

CHRISTOPHER NOXON writes essays, articles, and other stuff for *The New York Times,* Salon.com, and NPR. He's the author of *Rejuvenile: Kickball, Cartoons, Cupcakes, and the Reinvention of the American Grown-up.* Clips and such can be found at www.christophernoxon.com.

BRETT PAESEL is the author of the *Los Angeles Times* bestseller *Mommies Who Drink: Sex, Drugs, and Other Distant Memories of an Ordinary Mom,* as well as Meagan McPhee's fictional blog at www.firstwivesworld.com and a monthly beauty column for *Wondertime* magazine. As an actress she appeared in *Six Feet Under, Curb Your Enthusiasm,* and *The Gilmore Girls.*

NEAL POLLACK is the author of the bestselling memoir *Alternadad* and the founder of Offsprung.com, an online humor magazine. He's also written several books of satirical fiction, including the cult classic *The Neal Pollack Anthology of American Literature*, and has contributed to nearly every English-language publication in the world. He lives in Los Angeles with his wife, Regina Allen, and their son, Elijah.

JOAN RATER is a co–executive producer of *Grey's Anatomy* as well as proud mom to Maggie and Sally.

MARTA RAVIN is an Emmy-nominated television producer, writer, and comedian. As a stand-up comic and host she has appeared on Comedy Central, NBC, VH1, Bravo, and Oxygen. She lives in New York City with her husband, Max Leinwand, and their son, Jonah.

JULIE ROTTENBERG was a playwright before becoming a writer/ producer for HBO's *Sex and the City*. She currently lives in Brooklyn, where she writes for film and television with her writing partner, Elisa Zuritsky.

LEW SCHNEIDER has cobbled together a career as a comedian, game show host, actor, and TV writer. He received two Emmy awards for his work on *Everybody Loves Raymond* and hardly a thank-you for the years of parenting he's put into raising his three sons (with his wife, Liz Abbe, who really handles all the complicated stuff).

TOM SHILLUE is a writer and stand-up comedian whose many television appearances include his own Comedy Central stand-up special, *Late Night with Conan O'Brien*, and a segment on *The Daily Show with Jon Stewart*. His autobiographical monologues have gained a loyal following, and he shares a lot of his work freely at www.tomshillue.com.

MIKE SIKOWITZ has been a writer/producer for television comedies for almost two decades, including *Friends*, *Grounded for Life*, and *Rules of Engagement*. He lives in Los Angeles with his beloved wife, Bonnie, and their beautiful boys, Dov and Reed.

JOHANNA STEIN is a writer/director/comedian who splits her time between Los Angeles and Chicago, where she lives with her husband, David, and their pacifier-addicted daughter, Sadie. For an update on her non-breast-feeding breasts, go to www.johannastein.com.

TODD WARING is an actor and a writer. Some of his recent credits include appearances on *Nip/Tuck* and *Desperate Housewives*, as well as a political rant entitled "I'm Mad as Hell and Have to Take It for a Long, Long Time." More comic notions can be found on his Web site, at www.littleshopofhahas.com.

ERIC WEINBERG is a television writer whose credits include *Politically Incorrect with Bill Maher*, *Scrubs*, and *Californication*. He'd like to send love and thanks to his wife, Hilary, their sons, Benjamin and Julian, his sister, Patricia, and his parents, Hank and Sue, who would much rather brag to their friends about this book than about *Californication*.

MATTHEW WEINER recently won his third and fourth Emmy awards, for creating and writing the series *Mad Men*. Before that, he was executive producer of *The Sopranos*. He feels most fortunate to be married to his wife, Linda, and to get to spend his free time with his four sons, Marten, Charlie, Arlo, and Ellis.

MARCIA WILKIE has written for television talk shows, reality and game shows, and commercials, as well as for radio, and coauthored the *New York Times* bestselling book *Behind the Smile*, with Marie Osmond. Visit www.marciawilkie.com.

MOON UNIT ZAPPA is a comic and an actress. Her TV credits include *Curb Your Enthusiasm* and *Private Practice*. She lives in Los Angeles with her husband, Paul Doucette, and their daughter, Matilda.